I N V E S T I G A Ç Ã O

I|U

COEDIÇÃO

Imprensa da Universidade de Coimbra
Email: imprensa@uc.pt
URL: http//www.uc.pt/imprensa_uc
Vendas online: http://livrariadaimprensa.uc.pt
UNINT University Press

COORDENAÇÃO EDITORIAL

Imprensa da Universidade de Coimbra

CONCEÇÃO GRÁFICA

Imprensa da Universidade de Coimbra

IMAGEM DA CAPA

A group of students. Photo undated but attributed to the first decade of the 20th century.

INFOGRAFIA

Mickael Silva

EXECUÇÃO GRÁFICA

KDP

ISBN

978-989-26-2614-7

ISBN DIGITAL

978-989-26-2615-4

DOI

https://doi.org/10.14195/978-989-26-2615-4

IRENE VAQUINHAS
MARIA MANUELA TAVARES RIBEIRO

STUDENTS AND STUDENT LIFE AT THE UNIVERSITY OF COIMBRA

INDEX

INTRODUCTION

Irene Vaquinhas
Maria Manuela Tavares Ribeiro

In recent years, there has been an increase in historiographical production on Portuguese university students in the 19th and 20th centuries, as well as international comparative analyses, particularly on academic sociability and traditions, political activism, protagonism, in opposition to the authoritarian and police regime of the Estado Novo, and student movements. With regard to the place of women in the academic world, the literature has focused on the access of pioneering women to universities, the obstacles and gender stereotypes that affect representations of work, and the methods of inclusion or exclusion in the various scientific subjects. This process has crossed borders and moved towards more global and transnational readings.

The social and political history of the student milieu is a field of study in which curiosity about the past has intensified and become more widespread, and this does not seem to be unrelated to the vigorous and widespread student mobilisations currently taking place around the world, at least since 2018. Protests and political resistance, collective demands and contestations, communication strategies and leadership, international solidarity networks, have all been the subject of reflection and parallels with more or less recent situations in time, although sometimes, due to a lack of critical perspective or poor contextualisation, the question of anachronism and the instrumentalisation of history is raised[1]. However, the issue is currently on the political agenda in many countries.

Less well known, but no less complex, are the forms and effectiveness of student recruitment in relation to educational reforms, academic profiles and careers, implications for public policy and elite formation, in short, essential elements of a social history of universities, political universes and contemporary Europe.

This work consists of two studies on the students of the University of Coimbra, from the end of the 18th century to the first decades of the 20th century, at the historical moment of the decline of the *ancien régime* and the transition to modernity. The main sources used were the manuscripts and printed documents kept in the Archive of the University of Coimbra, which were cross-referenced with other types of sources, especially the periodical press and memoirs, in order to provide precise and documented support for the observations and conclusions presented.

These studies were published in Portuguese in the journal *Ler História* in 2020 and 2023, after being scientifically reviewed: the first, in collaboration with Maria Manuela Tavares Ribeiro, under the title "Students of the University of Coimbra from the Pombaline Reform to the Foundation of the Republic, 1772-1910"[2] and the second, by Irene Vaquinhas, "Aurora, a rebellious student. Gender, intolerance and protest at the Faculty of Law of the University of

---

[1] Seia, G. A., & Cejudo Ramos, D. de J. – "Movimientos estudiantiles universitarios en América Latina, Asia y África. Contribuciones sociohistóricas para un campo de investigación en consolidación" – *CIAN-Revista De Historia De Las Universidades*, 27 (1). p. 6-14. https://doi.org/10.20318/cian.2024.8657

[2] "Os estudantes da Universidade de Coimbra da reforma pombalina à implantação da República, 1772-1910 / Students of the University of Coimbra from the Pombaline Reform to the Founding of the Republic, 1772-1910 / Les étudiants de l'Université de Coimbra de la réforme pombaline à la République, 1772-1910" (2020) - *Ler História*, nº 76. p. 55-79; https://doi.org/10.4000/lerhistoria.6642

Coimbra during the First Republic"[3]. This book takes up these works, expanded and deepened, and translated into English. It is illustrated with a series of images consisting of prints, photographs and postcards alluding to material and symbolic aspects of the daily life of university students during the period in question, taken from publications, little-known collections or private archives. The iconographic view allows us to see the spaces and places where students gathered, to capture youthful irreverence and forms of transgression, and to follow the evolution of academic dress, known as the cape and gown, which lost its ecclesiastical characteristics in the 20th century in favour of civil secularisation, becoming optional soon after the proclamation of the Republic[4]. A process that is part of the academic challenge to the institution and its traditions, and that goes hand in hand with the evolution of the symbolism of university rites themselves, as Luís Reis Torgal rightly observes when he states that "The liberal revolution brought with it the intention of secularising society and institutions"[5].

This work has benefited from the generous support of many people and institutions, to whom we express our deep gratitude: the Centre for the History of Society and Culture (FCT Project UIDB/00311/2020UI), in the person of its Scientific Coordinator, Prof. Dr. José Pedro de Matos Paiva; the Faculty of Arts and Humanities of the University of Coimbra (Translation Support Fund), through its Director, Prof. Dr. Albano António Cabral Figueiredo, for the financial support for the English translations and for the direct contribution to the research; Dr. Ana Maria Bandeira, superior technique at the

---

[3] "Aurora, uma estudante insubmissa. Género, intolerância e contestação na Universidade de Coimbra na I República"- (2023) - *Ler História*, nº 83. p. 145-167; https://doi.org/10.4000/lerhistoria.12819

[4] Luís Reis Torgal - "Quid petis? Os doutoramentos na Universidade de Coimbra" (1993) - *Revista de História das Ideias*, vol. 15. p. 219.

[5] Luís Reis Torgal - *art. cit.*. p. 205.

University of Coimbra Archive, for providing us with the academic police file of Aurora Teixeira de Castro, and for her constant and kind availability to clarify the "collection" of the University of Coimbra, which she knows so well; Dr. Alexandre Ramires for the photographs from his private archive, some of them unpublished, which he generously provided and were essential for illustrating this work; the BLX-Lisbon Periodicals Library (Hemeroteca Municipal de Lisboa) for scanning and lending photographs from certain Periodicals; the Academic Museum of the University of Coimbra – Science Museum of the University of Coimbra for providing us with images of some pieces from their collection.

We would like to thank all those who have encouraged us to study the social history of the University of Coimbra, our *alma mater*.

This work seeks to understand and question various aspects of the historical legacy of the students of the University of Coimbra in the 19th and 20th centuries, bearing in mind that, no matter how scientific we try to be, the universe of certainties is uncontrollably fragile...

Students of the University of Coimbra
(18th-19th centuries)

1 – Student of the University of Coimbra. Source: Faculty of Arts and Humanities (University of Coimbra), Sala Ferreira Lima, Regional Costumes Box (18th-19th centuries)

2 – Student of the University of Coimbra. Source: Faculty of Arts and Humanities (University of Coimbra), Sala Ferreira Lima, Regional Costumes Box

3 – Student of the University of Coimbra. Source: Faculty of Arts and Humanities (University of Coimbra), Sala Ferreira Lima, *Album de Costumes Portuguezes*, David Corazzi Editor, 1888, Fasc. nº 5. According to the writer Ramalho Ortigão, who signed the text accompanying Alfredo Roque Gameiro's watercolour, the academic dress of the Coimbra University student depicted in the engraving had already fallen into disuse. This change seems to have taken place towards the end of the 19th century, when the shorts, high socks, headdress and lapel were replaced by a collar, tie and trousers, while the gown (or 'abatina') and cape were retained.

4 – Students of the University of Coimbra (late 19th century).
Source: Faculty of Arts and Humanities (University of Coimbra), Sala Ferreira Lima, Palhares Collection, Regional Costumes Box

5 – Postcard of a 20th century student of the University of Coimbra. Source: Faculty of Arts and Humanities (University of Coimbra), Sala Ferreira Lima, Regional Costumes Box.

6 – Postcard with a caricature of a student of the University of Coimbra.
Source: Faculty of Arts and Humanities (University of Coimbra), Sala Ferreira Lima, Portuguese Characters Postcards; Regional Costumes Box.

Daily life and student sociabilities

Vida de Coimbra

Na rua das Flôres, viela tortuosa onde existem quasi exclusivamente «republicas»

Distraindo-se.

346

7 and 8 – Aspects of daily student life in the city of Coimbra: in a street of "repúblicas", at the "alta universitária", and at the Café Montanha, a place of leisure and student socializing.

uma verruma para quando a sêde apertasse e não houvesse torneira. Ir ao cinematografo e colher um dos mais bizarros afetos da vida coimbrã: algazarra, comentarios picarescos, troças e namoros, tudo quanto é possivel esperar d'uma assoisse de moços sem trabalho. Certo, como tudo o mais, a plateia dos teatros de Coimbra vive longe dos tempos da Ristori; mas ainda no meu tempo ela ergueu em delirio algumas grandes nigromantes do proscénio e a Mimi não a lembra sem saudade. Depois do cine, começa a noite boémia. Desde que o Bossa levou para Coimbra a sua morbidez e a sua «sensiblerie» exgotuda, raros ousaram manter fidelidade á boémia portugueza d'outras éras. Todavia o «Magrinho» é ainda um refugio e eu não desisto de brindar com bacalhau e grêlos, n'uma ceia de risos inflorada, certa magrinha e doente amante da minha imaginação que breve lá irá colher aplausos de alguns que a meu pedido hão-de aplaudi-la...

1. O café Montanha que os estudantes preferem.—2. Lagôa na Portela.—(«Clichés» Garcez).

Noites de Coimbra, quem as soube viver a hautos plenos, no coração as traz eternamente... Possa alguem descrevêl-as que eu não sei.

João do Amaral.

Source: BLX-Lisbon Periodicals Library, João do Amaral, "Vida de Coimbra", *Ilustração Portuguesa*, Series II, nr 421, March 16 1914.

9 – A group of students. Photo undated but attributed to the first decade of the 20th century.

Source: Alexandre Ramires Private Archive, Casa Fotográfica Pinho Henriques Sucessor, Coimbra.

0 – A small group of students in a burlesque pose (early 20th century)

Source: Alexandre Ramires Private Archive, Casa Fotográfica Foto União, Coimbra, by José Gomes Tinoco.

11 – A group of students in the courtyard of the Schools (Pátio das Escolas), next to Via Latina (Faculty of Law), in the first decade of the 20th century. Octaviano do Carmo e Sá (1884-1956), a law student at the time, can be seen in the centre, on a bench, in a theatrical pose.

He would later become a lawyer and dedicate himself to the study of academic and popular traditions, especially in Coimbra.
Source: Alexandre Ramires Private Archive.

12 and 13 – Postcards alluding to a traditional and mythical theme in Coimbra's academic universe: the love affairs between students and "tricanas" (women from lower social classes).

As the number of female students increased, these "traditional affairs" tended to fade and disappear.
Source: Faculty of Arts and Humanities (University of Coimbra), Sala Ferreira Lima, Regional Costumes Box.

The 1907 academic strike and political protest

14 and 15 – Photos of the 1907 academic strike: near the Porta Férrea and the Arcos dos Jardim, in Coimbra

A' Porta Ferrea—Ao centro o filho do sr. presidente do conselho, Frederico Franco, que adheriu á gréve —Os estudantes de direito: srs. Luciano Henriques, Gonçalves Preto, expulso por um anno, e Jacintho Freitas (*Cliché da Phot. Gonçalves, de Coimbra.*)—Refractarios á photographia!—A cavallaria contendo os estudantes do lyceu, nos Arcos do Jardim, no dia 10 de abril—(*Clichés* de Benoliel, enviado especial da *Illustração Portugueza* a Coimbra)

Source: BLX- Lisbon Periodicals Library, *A Illustração Portuguesa*, 22 April 1907.

Nas horas calmas da greve

16 – Photo of striking students (1907 strike).

Junto à Porta Férrea um grupo de «grevistas», entre os quais se vêem os Drs. Deodoro de Castro Carneiro, Vergílio Correia Pinto da Fonseca, Luiz Baldaque Guimarães, Ladislau Patrício, João da Costa Cabedo, Henrique Braz e António Granjo, esperam pacìficamente o desenrolar dos acontecimentos

Source: Alexandre Ramires Private Archive, Joseph Benoliel; Rocha Martins, *Arquivo Gráfico da Vida Portuguesa: 1903-1918* (1933). Lisboa: Bertrand. p. 185.

17 – Polychrome ceramic plate with a student and a Coimbra tricana in the centre and the University in the background. The border shows symbols of academic hazing: wooden spoon, scissors, etc. Dated 1928, it belonged to fourth-year law students.
Source: Academic Museum of the University of Coimbra – Science Museum of the University of Coimbra

Students and Professors

18 – Photomontage of the poet João de Deus (1830-1890) in his student days (1850s), by fellow student Pedro Róxa.

Source: Alexandre Ramires Private Archive.

19 – Photo of the writer José Francisco Trindade Coelho (1861-1908), then a student at the Faculty of Law, ca. 1883.
Source: Alexandre Ramires Private Archive. Casa Fotográfica de José Maria dos Santos, Coimbra.

20 – Photo of António Macedo Papança (1852-1913), 1st Count of Monsaraz, then a student at the Faculty of Law, ca. 1874. Source: Alexandre Ramires Private Archive. Casa Fotográfica de Luís de Albuquerque, Coimbra.

21 – Photo of Domingos Fezas Vital (1888-1953), professor at the Faculty of Law. Photo undated, but attributed to the 1910s.
Source: Alexandre Ramires Private Archive. Photo by Gabriel Tinoco, photographer from Coimbra.

CARNEIRO PACHECO

Eis uma escala zoologica
De fazer pasmar a gente:
De carneiro *foi a* urso;
Hoje é urso, *amanhã...* lente!

22 – Caricature of António Faria de Carneiro Pacheco, professor at the Faculty of Law (1887-1957), dated 1910.
Source: Alexandre Ramires Private Archive, *Quid petis? Recordações dum quintanista. Caricatures by J. Valério (1910)*. Coimbra: F. França & Arménio Amado Editores. p. 5.

Women at the University of Coimbra

23 – Photo of Domitila Hormizinda Miranda de Carvalho (1871-1966) with fellow students. She was the first woman to attend the University of Coimbra continuously. In the academic year 1891-1892, she enrolled in the mathematics course, which she completed in 1894, and in 1895 and 1904 she graduated in philosophy and medicine.
Source: Alexandre Ramires Private Archive.

Group photo of law students with only one woman. Undated photo, but attributed to the 2nd decade of the 20th century.

Source: Alexandre Ramires Private Archive.

25 – Photo of Aurora de Castro Gouveia. In Arnaldo Brazão, *O Primeiro Congresso Feminista e de Educação (Relatorio)* (1925), Lisboa: Ed. Spartacus. p. 82.

SR.ª D. REGINA QUINTANILHA *a primeira senhora portugueza que exerce a advocacia, tendo-se estreiado brilhantemente ha dias no tribunal da Boa Hora* — (Cliché Vasques)

II Série — N.º 405 **Ilustração Portugueza** *Lisboa, 24 de Novembro de 1913*

DIRÉTOR E PROPRIETARIO J. J. DA SILVA GRAÇA
EDITOR: JOSÉ JOUBERT CHAVES

EDIÇÃO SEMANAL DO JORNAL O SECULO

Assinatura para Portugal, colonias portuguezas e Hespanha:

Redação, administração, offic. de composição e impressão
RUA DO SECULO, 43

Trimestre...... 1$20 cent. Semestre...... 2$40 cent.
Ano...... 4$80 cent. Numero avulso. 10 cent.

26 – Regina Quintanilha, the first female student at the Faculty of Law (1910-1911), when she started working at the Boa Hora Court in Lisbon in 1913. Source: BLX-Lisbon Periodicals Library, *Ilustração Portugueza*, II série, nº 405, 24 November 1913.

27 – Ceramic figure of a female student of the University of Coimbra. The academic costume consists only of the cape, and in her hand she holds a briefcase with yellow ribbons, indicating that she attended the Faculty of Medicine (1st half of the 20th century). Legislation in 1924 extended the use of the academic costume to higher education and secondary school students. The beginning of its use by women is dated to the 1950s. Source: Academic Museum of the University of Coimbra – Science Museum of the University of Coimbra

Students of the University of Coimbra from the Pombaline Reform to the Founding of the Republic, 1772-1910

Irene Vaquinhas
https://orcid.org/0000-0003-1889-165X

Maria Manuela Tavares Ribeiro
https://orcid.org/0000-0001-7471-2164

Abstract
The University of Coimbra (Portugal) clearly captivated successive generations of students, who considered it the institution of the future elites and a means to rise to power. Who attended Coimbra as a student? Who were these youths, and what motivated them? This article analyses the student body between 1772 and 1910 from several angles, taking into account the historical context and the students' socio-economic profiles. It aims to show continuities and discontinuities, sometimes even the breakdown of an academic career. Coimbra students in that period mostly came from a bourgeois background. The University can thus be considered to have been elitist. Based on information regarding the geographical and social origin, the daily routines, and the components of the student experience, the article comes to profiling the average student, the

connection to university and urban life, and their social and political strength.

Keywords
University of Coimbra, students, university life, Coimbra academia.

Introduction

In his work *Noutros Tempos*, António Aurélio da Costa Ferreira describes his arrival in Coimbra to enrol at university in 1902 as follows:

> Coimbra fascinated me. My head was filled with a thousand stories of academic pranks and exploits. Thirsting for freedom, already of a very revolutionary mind, I was making my way, despite my quiet, shy nature, thanks to my uncle, [...] devising plans for a revolutionary life and the outlines of an outstanding oeuvre. A first-year aspiring to be someone, in my mind's seye, I saw Coimbra as a colossal chicken hatching great men[1].

It is impossible to deny the fascination that Coimbra has exerted over generation after generation of students. Prior to the founding of the Universities of Lisbon and Porto in 1911, Coimbra was the country's leading academic institution. In this regard, time spent in the city, which is evoked with nostalgia in countless memoirs, represented an important stage in the lives of thousands of young people who, though they may have temporarily protested against the idea, aspired to become members of the ruling elite. In fact, admission to one of Europe's oldest universities, which was officially considered one

[1] António Aurélio da Costa Ferreira - *Noutros Tempos*. Coimbra: Livraria Neves Editora, 1915. p. 51-52.

of the seedbeds for the ruling class and political and administrative positions, attracted a mass of young people who recognised the titles and diplomas awarded by the institution as a mechanism necessary for the social reproduction of the ruling classes, and one of the few paths available to access power civilly. Though undergraduate and doctoral degrees remained very restricted in number, merely enrolling at the university was enough to gain unique status within Portugal, with students developing a feeling of belonging to an exclusive, privileged group, which gave them a firm 'feeling of superiority'[2]. Group identity was sanctioned by a specific subculture, defined by its own traditions, practices, clothing, slang, heroes, neighbourhoods, and the like, aided the building of social bridges between newcomers – *caloiros*, or freshmen, less commonly known as *novatos*, or novices – while also contributing to the student population being identified in an urban context. Certain forms of rivalry between students and non-students, particularly the *futricas*[3], emphasised this differentiation and worked to bring the group even closer together and enhancing its self-esteem.

An ideological frame of reference that imposed itself throughout the nineteenth century under the influence of the Romantic movement graced students with a certain cultural independence, allowing them to assert themselves politically. Whether enlisting in the battalions of academia or skipping classes to form 'human walls' of protest, applauding loudly or holding silent demonstrations, composing heroic-comedic poems or starting riots outside the Sala dos Capelos, students were an important social and political force in the period between the Pombaline Reform and the Republic[4]. Indeed, student

---

[2] Maria Eduarda Cruzeiro, *Action symbolique et formation scolaire.L'Université de Coimbra et sa Faculté de Droit dans la seconde moitié du XIXe siècle* (1990) (doctoral thesis in 2 vols.). Paris, vol. 1. p. 132-139. The translations provided are our own.

[3] The name given to Coimbra locals external to academia.

[4] For a detailed chronology of the key student movements during the period from 1772 to 1910, see among others Alberto Sousa Lamy - *A Academia de Coimbra*

activism helped instil liberalism and, later, republicanism[5], having played an active role in the establishment of a constitutional state. It is not always easy, however, to dissociate political motivations from specifically academic goals, nor have such movements always operated in reaction against tradition and the prevailing regime[6].

Literary sources, specifically memoirs written by former students, painted a vague, abstract portrait of a Coimbra student, who was characterised by a taste for bohemia and nonsense, hazing, and an apparent lack of commitment to studying. A timeless image, it transcends all social and historical differences and is based on a mythical representation of student life, linked to the idea of freedom and the absence of pressure from family and the community. However, this pattern of behaviour could hardly be adhered to by a large proportion of the young people who sought to attend the University of Coimbra. The relatively strict measures applied to entrance exams for various subjects[7], the attendance requirements[8], the living and accommodation costs in the city, and the progressively scientific nature of the studies – all factors that were particularly sensitive

1537-1990. História, praxe, boémia e estudo, partidas e piadas, organismos académicos (1990). Lisbon. p. 48-182.

[5] On student involvement in the republican movement, see Ana Maria Caiado Boavida - "Tópicos sobre a prática política dos estudantes republicanos, 1890-1931: limites e condicionalismos do movimento estudantil" (1983). *Análise Social*, vol. XIX, 77-78-79, and Luís Reis Torgal - "Universidade de Coimbra". In *Dicionário de História da I República e do Republicanismo*, vol. 3. Lisbon: Assembleia da República, 2013. p. 1053-1060.

[6] Luís Reis Torgal - "Universidade de Coimbra" (2013). In *Dicionário de História da I República e do Republicanismo*, vol. 3. Lisbon: Assembleia da República. p. 1053-1060.

[7] On this matter, among other legislative measures see the ordinance of 13 September 1848 amending the regulation on entrance exams for the university's scientific courses, in order 'to cease the indulgence and relaxation that may have occurred in these exercises': *Legislação académica coligida pelo Dr. José Maria de Abreu. Coordenada, revista e ampliada pelo Dr. António dos Santos Viegas*, vol. 1 [1772-1850] (1894). Coimbra. p. 340-341.

[8] *Regulamento para a fiscalização e julgamento das faltas dos estudantes da Universidade de Coimbra* (1904). Coimbra: Imprensa da Universidade.

from the mid-nineteenth century onwards – made it difficult for the student, however timeless, to come into being. Who, after all, was the 'academic youth'? The answer to this question is not easy, nor can a concrete answer be given. The acute subjectivity of some sources, and the voluminous nature of others, heightened by the length of the period under analysis, make it difficult to objectively and rigorously define student society between 1772 and 1910. As such, a methodology was chosen that allows for academic context to be traced, albeit at a large scale, by privileging quantitative sources so as to ascertain the strengths of the socio-economic profiles of the students in attendance at the university, highlighting the continuities and ruptures of each academic trajectory.

Certidões de Idade, or Age Certificates – documents required of university candidates for enrolment – were the primary source for this research. These were then cross-referenced with other types of information, whenever possible, with a particular focus on the academic years 1780-81, 1836-37, 1861-62 and 1909-10. This selection of dates is not entirely arbitrary. The choice was made to avoid phases of greater political instability during the nineteenth century, the effects of which on academic life are all too well known. This criterion does not exclude the possibility of distortions in the records, whether due to conjunctions or to circumstances inherent to university life itself. However, it does present the undeniable advantage of allowing for the coverage of a period of more than a one hundred years. In addition to these documents, found in the Archive of the University of Coimbra (UCA), the following were also used: Assessments and Degrees (1785-88), Exams (1772-73 and 1789-90), Doctoral Defences and Degrees (1772-84) for the academic year 1780-81; the second volume of Age Certificates (1834-1900), the Student List (1836) for the year 1836-37; and the Student List (1862) – according to data collected by António Madeira, to whom the authors are grateful – for the academic year 1861-1862; Processes and Enrolment, Age Certificates (1909-10), Enrolment Books (1909-10) and an Annual Publication (1910) for the academic year 1909-10[9].

We turn to questioning the sources and some of the issues considered fundamental to studying university populations, according to Laurence Stone: Who were the students and how many were there? What jobs did they fill?[10]

1. Enrolment and attendance patterns

António de Vasconcelos estimated the number of students who attended the University of Coimbra between the academic years of 1800-01 and 1900-01 at 91,888, having arrived at this figure by counting the students registered in Enrolments Books kept in the Archive of the University of Coimbra[11]. This number is, however, exaggerated, since it overestimates the size of the student population[12]. In fact, studies carried out by Maria Eduarda Cruzeiro and Manuel Alberto Carvalho Prata using the nominative lists of students transcribed in the university Yearbook (*Anuário da Universidade*) for the periods of 1868-1910 and 1880-1926, respectively, produced numbers 20 to 30 per cent lower[13]. As such, enrolment numbers inflate student numbers by about a third of their actual figure (Table 1).

---

[9] This documentation is supplemented with additional sources identified in the text.

[10] John M. Burney - *Toulouse et son Université. Facultés et étudiants dans la France provinciale du 19e siècle* (1988). Paris: CNRS-Presses Universitaires du Mirail. p. 20.

[11] António de Vasconcelos (1941) - "Estatística dos estudantes matriculados na Universidade de Coimbra durante o século XIX, e dos graus de licenciado e de doutor nela conferidos no mesmo século, isto é, desde 1 de Janeiro de 1801 até 31 de Dezembro de 1900". *Escritos Vários*. Coimbra: Coimbra Editora Lda, vol. 2.

[12] On the main gaps in enrolment for research on students, see, among others, Margarita Torremocha Hernández (1995) - "La población estudiantil de la Universidad de Oñate, Siglo XVII". *Investigaciones Históricas*, nº 15. p. 213-218.

[13] Maria Eduarda Cruzeiro (1990) - *Action symbolique et formation scolaire: l'Université de Coimbra et la Faculté de Droit dans la seconde moitié du XIXe siècle*, Paris. p. 522, and Manuel Alberto Carvalho Prata (1994) - *A Academia de Coimbra*

Table 1. Comparison of the number of enrolments and students (1868-1908)

Year	A Enrolments	B Students	C Students
1868	779	–	599
1870	801	–	609
1872	953	–	723
1874	903	–	705
1876	864	–	649
1878	794	–	581
1880	766	573	571
1882	818	605	604
1884	958	673	673
1886	1115	774	774
1888	1126	810	813
1890	1180	872	873
1892	1200	905	905
1894	1240	948	948
1896	1306	1021	1021
1898	1419	1084	1118
1900	1449	1181	1181
1902	–	1027	1028
1904	–	920	911
1906	–	1050	1050
1908	–	1190	1195

Sources: A –Vasconcelos, 'Estatística dos estudantes matriculados na Universidade de Coimbra', vol. 2; B – Cruzeiro, *Action symbolique et formation scolaire*, vol. 2. p. 522; C – Prata, *A Academia de Coimbra*, vol. 2. p. 57-58.

The discrepancy between the results can be explained by the use of different sources and research methods. In fact, student records were artificially multiplied by the attendance of modules common

*(1880-1926). Sociedade, cultura e política (*1994). Vol. 2, Coimbra: Univ. doctoral thesis. p. 57-58; Maria Eduarda Cruzeiro (1988) - "A reforma pombalina na história da Universidade". *Análise Social*. XXIV, 100, 1°. p. 166.

to more than one school, as well as by the requirement that, from the third year of the Mathematics course and in the last three years of the Philosophy course, enrolment was registered by module. This meant that the numbers registered did not correspond to realistic numbers of individuals. Using a coefficient that allows for enrolment statistics to be corrected to obtain a number that is as close as possible to the actual student population has been advantageous when used by other authors in similar studies[14].

The main difficulty, however, is to specify the appropriate correction rate, given that this varies according to the average length of university studies and course structures, among other factors. It is important to emphasise that between the Pombaline Reform and the founding of the Republic, the structures of the courses run by the various faculties were subject to several instances of restructuring. With modules either added or removed, and general course lengths either increased or reduced, these alterations had inevitable repercussions on the volume of enrolments, making it challenging to calculate the coefficient to be adopted[15]. Only a systematic and nominative survey of all students – carried out by comparing enrolments – would make it possible to eliminate double registrations and calculate the total number of students that made up the academic population[16]. However,

---

[14] William Frijhoff (1986). "Grandeur des nombres et misères des réalités: la courbe de Franz Eulenburg et le débat sur le nombre d'intellectuels en Allemagne, 1576-1815", in D. Julia, J. Revel, and R. Chartier (eds.), *Les universités européennes du XVIe au XVIIIe siècle. Histoire sociale des populations étudiantes.* vol. 1. Paris: École des Hautes Études en Sciences Sociales.

[15] Among the restructurings that took place, one should single out the royal charter of 21 December 1793, which modified the Theology course structure, besides the reform of higher education promulgated by Passos Manuel, on 5 December 1836, which changed the structure of the courses taught at the university and created the School of Law, after the merger of the Faculties of Law and Canon Law in *Memoria Professorum Universitatis Conimbrigensis. 1772-1937* (1992). ed. Manuel Augusto Rodrigues, vol. 2, Coimbra: AUC. p. 3-5, 89, 135-40, 181-85, 245-49, 319.

[16] The nominative register of first year students from 1780-81, 1836-37, 1861-62 and 1909-10, shows that the average enrolment per student was 1.01, 1.24, 1.14 and 1.31, respectively, meaning that the students and enrolments did not coincide

pending the publication of this fundamental documentation, which is currently being digitised – despite the shortcomings noted, which require caution when used to draw conclusions and weigh results – enrolment records do enable the general characteristics of the student population to be estimated. They reinforce the idea that enrolments adequately expressed university attendance trends, with a significantly close correlation between the two time-specific data series (r=0.985).

Judging by the same source, the number of enrolments increased significantly during the nineteenth century, particularly from the 1880s onwards. However, the numbers fluctuated, reflecting the political, social, and demographic instability that characterised the first half of the nineteenth century (Graph 1). During the century's early years, enrolments registered significant variations from year to year, which is partially justified by the interruption of academic activities due to the closure of the university following the French invasions, liberal struggles, and the Revolution of Maria da Fonte[17]. However, the impact of these events on student attendance was not even, nor did students fail to attend university entirely. It was not until the 1830s that enrolment numbers saw a significant decline, reaching the lowest numbers registered throughout the entire century. During that decade, the average annual enrolment fell to about half of what it had been in previous decades (470 in 1831-40 versus 875, 904, and 1,057 in 1800-01, 1811-20 and 1821-30, respectively)[18], a fact that cannot be separated from the university closure that took place in

---

in number, except for in 1780-81 when the tallies practically overlapped (98.8 per cent). In the remaining academic years, the percentage of students registering one enrollment only decreased, reaching 80.6 per cent in 1836-37; 87.5 per cent in 1861-62; and 76.2 per cent in 1909-10.

[17] The university was closed in the academic years 1810-11, 1828-29, 1831-32, 1832-33, 1833-34 and 1846-47.

[18] A list of enrolments, divided into ten-year periods, from 1790 to 1900, can be found in Maria Eduarda Cruzeiro - *Action symbolique et formation scolaire ... ob. cit.*. tome 2. p. 525.

1831-34, during which students joined academic battalions that set off on military expeditions. To this should be added the demographic impact of the cholera epidemic of 1833, which, coinciding with the civil war between Liberals and Miguelites, negatively affected the normal growth of the Portuguese population[19].

Graph 1. The general pattern of enrolments
(real numbers and moving averages)

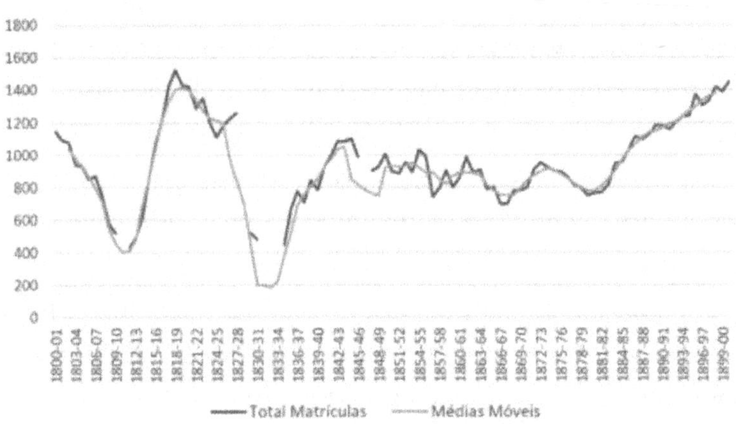

Source: Vasconcelos, 'Estatística dos estudantes matriculados na Universidade de Coimbra'.

Once the crisis had been overcome and the political situation stabilised, university life also returned to normal, with the enrolment figures returning to those registered prior to the period of turbulence. These fluctuated between 800 to 900 enrolled students per year, a number that remained unchanged until 1880. In the last quarter of the nineteenth century, the number of enrolments and

19 Rui Cascão (1993). "Demografia e sociedade". in J. Mattoso (ed.). *História de Portugal*. vol. 5 – O Liberalismo. Coord. Luís Reis Torgal; João Lourenço Roque, Lisbon: Editorial Estampa. p. 426.

students increased slightly, surpassing one-thousand in 1896. In that year, the University of Coimbra registered a total of 1,021 students, with the annual attendance remaining around this number until the establishment of the Republic (Table 1). The first woman was also allowed to enrol at the university to pursue higher education during this period, in the academic year 1890-1891[20], although some women had been taking specialist Pharmacy exams since the 1860s[21]. The unprecedented nature of these requests forced the rector of the university to ask for instructions from higher up on how to proceed, and a decree was issued by the Ministry of the Kingdom, dated 25 October 1869, in which the acceptance of the request was based on "|...| the example of the most advanced nations where both sexes are guaranteed the right to practise the art of healing and where there are even very distinguished women |...|" and that "...| there is no law in the country prohibiting women from studying medicine or pharmacy, nor is the pharmaceutical practice incompatible with the female sex"[22]. Domitila de Carvalho had also requested authorisation to enrol at the university, which was granted by the Minister of Public Instruction and Fine Arts, with the "exemption from wearing the academic costume, but obliging her to present herself in class and in all academic acts honestly dressed in black, with a suit appropriate to her sex", since the cape and gown were

---

[20] Joaquim Ferreira Gomes (1986) - "As primeiras mulheres que frequentaram a Universidade de Coimbra (1891-1910)". In *Boletim do Arquivo da Universidade de Coimbra*. VIII. p. 143-257; Joaquim Ferreira Gomes (1987) - *A mulher na Universidade de Coimbra*. Coimbra: Livraria Almedina. p. 9-23; Luís Reis Torgal - "Universidade de Coimbra", *art. cit.*. p. 1053.

[21] Ana Maria Leitão Bandeira and João Rui Rocha Pita (1990) - "As primeiras mulheres farmacêuticas na Universidade de Coimbra". In *Kalliope. De medicina*. N° 3. p. 21-28; Irene Vaquinhas (2018) - "Mulheres na universidade de Coimbra: o caso das primeiras estudantes cabo-verdianas' / 'Women at the University of Coimbra: the case of the first Cape Verdean female students". In *História. Revista da FLUP*, 4th series, VIII. 1. 2018. p. 225-227.

[22] UCA, Processes for academic degrees licences (SR), 3rd series, box 68 (Pharmacy, 1869).

for the exclusive use of male students[23]. However, the presence of women at the university would remain low, even though some of the more enlightened sectors of public opinion, mainly linked to republican circles, were in favour of this advance. Nevertheless, its impact on the student body was negligible until the proclamation of the Portuguese Republic (1910)[24]. As for women's admission to the Faculty of Law, which was one of the later schools to admit women, this did not take place until after 1910. Despite the progress made in the field of women's education, the title 'university student' still applied almost entirely to male students.

Generally speaking, only a modest increase was seen in the number of students registered throughout the nineteenth century, similar to other European countries with Catholic traditions whose populations were strongly influenced by the French Revolution and the rise of liberalism[25]. The proportion of students of higher education in the total male population of mainland Portugal and the islands remained very low, at around three to four students per ten thousand inhabitants (Table 2)[26], placing Portugal as a

[23] Joaquim Ferreira Gomes (1991) - "Domitila de Carvalho – a primeira mulher na Universidade de Coimbra". In *Estudos para a História da Universidade de Coimbra*. Coimbra. p. 41-42.

[24] According to data collected in Joaquim Ferreira Gomes (1987) - *A mulher na Universidade de Coimbra*. Coimbra. p. 25, the number of students who enrolled in the various courses run by the University of Coimbra until 1910 was twenty three. During the First Republic (1910-1926), their number increased to 297, in addition to twenty two students who attended various smaller courses; Ana Marcella de Carvalho (2019) - *As mulheres na Universidade de Coimbra ao tempo da Primeira República (1910-1926)*. Coimbra: FLUC (master's diss.). p. 42.

[25] In reference to France, Antoine Prost (1968) - *L'enseignement en France 1800-1967*. Paris: Armand Colin. p. 224, speaks of the 'long stagnation of the years 1800-1880'. For Spain, Mariano Peset and Jose Luis Peset (1974). *La Universidad Española (Siglos XVIII y XIX). Despotismo Ilustrado y Revolución Liberal*. Madrid: Taurus Ediciones, S. A.. p. 531, mentions the considerable drop in the number of students during the liberal period, followed by a slow recovery.

[26] These calculations were made by dividing the total number of students by the overall male population, as recorded in the population censuses of 1864, 1878, 1890, and 1900.

country with little progress compared to other nations. The balance is not, however, entirely negative. From 1878 to the end of the century, the university population grew consistently at an average annual rate of 3.45 and 3.06 per cent, between 1878 and 1890, and 1890 and 1900, respectively, and at a rate higher than that of male literacy, which remained at 1.25 and 1.53 per cent for these periods[27].

Table 2. Number of students at the University of Coimbra per ten thousand inhabitants

Year	A	B
1868	3	–
1878	3	11
1890	4	14
1900	6	16

Source: Population census (1864, 1878, 1890, 1900) Notes: A – relative to the total male population; B – relative to the total literate male population.

At first glance, the data suggest that the restructuring of higher education by Passos Manuel in 1836, which, among other things, led to the creation of polytechnic institutions, medical-surgical schools, and Pharmacy schools in the cities of Lisbon and Porto, had repercussions on attendance at the country's most prestigious institution, slowing down its natural growth. Providing technical and scientific education to prepare young people for the modern world, these educational institutions began to compete with the University of Coimbra, although the new professional careers pursued were geared to specific purposes. Indeed, the creation

[27] The calculations were made using the number of students listed in Cruzeiro. *Action symbolique et formation scolaire ... ob. cit.*. tome 2. p. 525, for the years 1878, 1890 and 1900, and from the calculations of the literate male population provided in the population censuses of 1878, 1890 and 1900.

of these institutions was part of a political framework aimed at breaking Coimbra's monopoly on education. However, these new courses did not rival the education provided by old institutions in terms of prestige and recognition, nor did they follow identical rules of socially based selection criteria, since university studies were reserved for the upper classes[28]. The institutional effects of Passos Manuel's decentralisation policy on higher education are still to be interpreted, particularly in terms of the resistance raised at Coimbra, a *university fortress*[29].

The overall impact of the liberal reforms can be considered to have negatively affected the university movement, resulting in a weak influx of students into the city of Coimbra. This conclusion is reinforced by the comparison with an 'apparent prosperity' during the late eighteenth century, as expressed in a sizeable 12,163 registrations[30] – a figure that would not be reached again until the 1890s. This is further illustrated by the relatively small number of students attending the university in the academic year of 1861-62, as reflected in the teacher-student ratio, which was then 12.11 (average term) for active teachers, or 10.62 if retired staff are included (Table 3). Finally, the crisis in higher education manifested itself in changes in the choice of university subject, which has altered the distribution of students across the university departments. This configured the academic framework from which the 'new higher education students' would emerge, bourgeois in their social origins and pragmatic in their goals.

---

[28] Maria Antonieta Cruz (1994) - *Os burgueses do Porto na segunda metade do século XIX*. Porto: Univ. doctoral thesis. p. 564, found that the students who attended the Polytechnic Academy of Porto in the academic year 1885-1886 came from more modest households than the average student of the University of Coimbra.

[29] Luís Reis Torgal (1987) - "Passos Manuel e a Universidade. Do Vintismo ao Setembrismo". *Cultura, História e Filosofia*, nº 6. p. 79-92.

[30] Maria Eduarda Cruzeiro - *Action symbolique et formation scolaire ... ob. cit.*. tome 2. p. 525.

Table 3. Teacher/student ratio in the year 1861-62, according to subject

	Students	Teachers		Ratio	
	Nr.	I	II	I	II
Law	464	24	27	19.33	17.19
Philosophy	114	11	14	10.36	8.14
Mathematics	124	14	15	8.86	8.27
Medicine	54	9	11	6.00	4.91
Theology	104	13	14	8.00	7.43
Total	860	71	81	12.11	10-62

Source: UCA, Payroll records (January 1862); Students from 1861-62.
Note: Column II includes retired teachers.

Where enrolment was concerned (see Table 4)[31], Law was by far the most popular subject, followed, though not closely, by scientific subjects (Mathematics and Philosophy), with Medicine registering relatively low levels of attendance. By contrast, Theology became less attractive over time, with enrolment numbers decreasing considerably throughout the nineteenth century, although this pattern was irregular with periods of descending numbers alternating with periods of stagnation and spells of recovery. The deterioration in the relationship between Church and State following the victory of liberalism was also reflected in education, curbing the social and cultural standing of religious studies. As a result, the Faculty of Theology suffered major setbacks before finally closing in 1911. Data collected from the certificates of students enrolled in

[31] Table 4 has been put together following the decennial calculations carried out in Cruzeiro. Maria Eduarda Cruzeiro - *Action symbolique et formation scolaire... ob. cit.*. tome 2. p. 525) for the period 1790-1799 to 1890-1900. The percentage of students attending each course is as follows: Law 52.3 per cent, Theology 5.2 per cent, Medicine 8.7 per cent, Mathematics 13.7 per cent, and Philosophy 20.1 per cent. The percentages provided for the last two courses do not correspond to the number of graduates from these faculties, reflecting the requirement for Medicine students to enrol in preparatory courses in the faculties of Philosophy (first year) and of Mathematics (first to third year).

the first year at all schools, from 1780-81, 1836-37, 1861-62 and 1909-10 confirm these trends, which were also reflected in other European institutions.

Table 4. Progression of enrolments of first-year students, by course

	1780-81	1836-37	1861-62	1910-11	Total
	%	%	%	%	%
Law	32.5*	45.7	43.6	34.8	37.8
Medicine	2.7	3.0	5.9	2.8	3.4
Mathematics	32.8	30.7	25.4	29.5	29.6
Philosophy	16.9	19.5	13.6	19.7	18.0
Mathematics / Philosophy	–	–	–	8.8	3.9
Theology	7.1	1.1	11.5	1.2	4.2
Pharmacy**	–	–	–	3.2	1.4
Undetermined	8.5	–	–	–	1.6
Total	100.0	100.0	100.0	100.0	100.0

Source: UCA, Age Certificates. Notes: (*) Sum of the Schools of Canon Law and Law; (**) Pharmacy course run by the School of Medicine elevated to the category of high-level course by charter dating 19 July 1902.

The circumstances seen in Coimbra can also be witnessed in the Catholic universities of Paris, Toulouse and Valencia, among others[32]. The most prominent schools specialised in jurisprudence – a trend that can be observed in earlier periods[33] – and produced generations of lawyers, magistrates, and other legal professionals who would play a decisive role in the transition from absolutism to liberalism and, later, in the consolidation of constitutional monarchies.

---

[32] John M. Burney - *Toulouse et son Université..., ob. cit.*. p. 149-182; Jean-Claude Caron (1991) - *Générations romantiques. Les étudiants de Paris et le Quartier Latin (1814-1851)*. Paris: Armand Colin. p. 43-47; Marc Baldó i Lacomba (1984) - *Profesores y estudiantes en la epoca romantica. La Universidad de Valencia en la crisis del Antiguo Regimen (1786-1843)*. Valencia. p. 86.

[33] Maria Rosa di Simone (1996) - "A admissão", In W. Ruëgg (ed.). *Uma história da Universidade na Europa*. Vol. 2, Lisbon. p. 297.

Law degrees were the best at enabling students to face the numerous issues arising from the newly-modified legal and political structures (including the abolition of the seigneurial system, the freeholding of land, depreciation of coinage, and so forth), in addition to being essential for building a career that could lead to the highest spheres of political governance[34]. As P. Bourdieu rightly points out in his classic study of the cultural sociology of the French university, *Homo academicus*, published in 1984, in which he uses various types of indicators, it is in the socially dominant faculties, such as the Faculty of Law, that the highest levels of political and economic power are observed[35]. This did not prevent a 'conflict between schools' from breaking out during certain periods – the Vintist period, for example – in which students took a critical stance towards legal studies, defending instead the importance of learning the sciences[36]. Exact science subjects, Medicine in particular, were not considered to be as relevant as those pertaining to Law. In Portugal, this could be attributed to competition from medical-surgical schools, namely in Lisbon and Porto, and somehow to the social disfavour of doctors and surgeons.

2. The social recruitment of students and their origins

Having established, in general terms, the ways in which educational institutions developed from the Pombaline reform to the Republic, the next step is to characterise the student body, attempting to out-

[34] Fátima Moura Ferreira (2010) - "Os juristas e a representação política". In F. Catroga and P. T. Almeida (eds.) - *Res publica. Cidadania e representação política em Portugal 1820-1926*. Lisbon. p. 217-25.

[35] See Luís Reis Torgal (1990) - "Universidade, conservadorismo e dinâmica de mudança". *Revista de História das Ideias*. n.° 12, Coimbra: IHTI/FLUC. p. 134, nt. 11.

[36] *Idem, ibidem*.

line its socio-economic profile and geographical origins. In a period during which Portuguese society was undergoing profound transformations as a result of the transition from absolutism to liberalism, the Portuguese university system had to produce a ruling elite and a culture adapted to the new economic and social conditions. Within these parameters, the University of Coimbra prioritised curricular reform. It also ensured the consistency of the social class of its recruits until the end of the nineteenth century. This is suggested by the analysis of Table 5, detailing the socio-professional background of the parents of students enrolled in the first year of the university in the academic years 1780-81, 1836-37, 1861-62, and 1910-11. However, the importance of the results gained should not be diminished by the high rate of unspecified backgrounds (over 75 per cent).

Table 5. Comparative socio-professional background of parents of first--year students

	1780-81		**1836-37**		**1861-62**		**1910-11**		**Total**	
	Nr.	%	Nr.	%	Nr.	%	Nr.	%	Nr.	%
University Graduates	19	6.48	21	9.81	19	7.57	29	5.57	88	6.88
Magistrates	4	1.37	5	2.34	9	3.59	15	2.88	33	2.58
Liberal professions	2	0.68	3	1.40	–	–	49	9.40	54	4.22
Military personnel	18	6.14	16	7.48	3	1.20	35	6.72	72	5.63
Nobility	2	0.68	3	1.40	4	1.59	–	–	9	0.70
Civil servants	3	1.02	1	0.47	–	–	65	12.5	69	5.39
Landowners and farmers	–	–	–	–	1	0.40	168	32.2	169	13.20
Traders and merchants	1	0.34			2	0.80	56	10.7	59	4.61
Industrialists and capitalists	–	–	–	–	–	–	13	2.50	13	1.02
Skilled manual labourers	1	0.34	–	–	–	–	20	3.84	21	1.64

Service workers	–	–	–	–	–	–	2	0.38	2	0.16
Others	–	–	–	–	–	–	4	0.77	4	0.31
Unspecified	243	82.90	165	77.10	213	84.90	65	12.5	686	53.6
Total	293	100	214	100	251	100	521	100	1279	100

Source: UCA, Age Certificates.

The social composition of the student body, divided into large groups, remained relatively homogeneous until the mid-19th century. Approximately 10 to 20 per cent of the students came from the middle or upper middle classes, with their parents' professions identified as university lecturers, magistrates and high-ranking military personnel, particularly with the rank of captain. The most prominent social category among those registered was higher education graduates, with licenciate degree holders predominating over other graduates, although this provides us with little information on the occupation subsequently chosen. Despite these omissions, it would seem that there is a continuity between the generations of university students, their social origin being repeated from parents to children, extending the professional trajectory of families. With this in mind, obtaining a higher education diploma cannot be considered to have been instrumental in promoting social mobility, which was probably achieved through other means (marriage, wealth, or inheritance). After all, many of the Portuguese bourgeoisie still preferred the honorary titles of baron or viscount, so often bestowed in exchange for political, military, and social support, to the prestigious status of lawyer or medical doctor.

By 1910, a significant change could already be noted in the professions of the parents of students, with the traditional sectors giving way to administrative professions, merchants, and traders and, most prominently, landowners and other agricultural occupations. How should this change be interpreted? As an indication of elite renewal? Or, quite the opposite, as a reflection of the broadening access to higher education for previously excluded social classes? The relatively narrow social milieu and small percentages do not, however, allow for conclusive answers. It seems reasonable, to admit that during the constitutional monarchy period university studies progressively became a privileged means of advancement for younger members of the bourgeoisie, promoted by the economic development brought about by the Regeneration. This phenomenon is in common to other European countries, justified by the emergence of industrial economies, the growing need for a technologically skilled workforce, the development of state administrations, and the secularisation of culture, among other factors[37].

In the specific case of Portugal, the primary beneficiaries of this relatively generalised meritocratic selection process were individuals whose background was relatively comfortable, and whose parents were placed in the middle rungs of the civil service or belonged to a middle-class rural bourgeoisie of landlords, farmers, and the like. These classes would have been financially able to allow their children to study at university, thanks to their relative economic well-being. For this emerging bourgeoisie, the University of Coimbra became a symbol of their pursuit of legitimacy, which came to involve the institution more and more.

The lower sectors of the petite bourgeoisie, the popular classes, were practically excluded from higher education despite their demographic weight. The most prolific profession within this 'world' of production and labour was that of the craftsmen. Thanks to special circumstances and a favourable conjuncture, they were able to guarantee a university education for their descendants. As for the children of servants, only exceptionally did they reach higher education. In fact, compulsory tuition fees and the high cost of schooling guaranteed social selectivity. This favoured students from more privileged

---

[37] John M. Burney - *Toulouse et son Université…, ob. cit.*. p. 171; Terry Shinn (1980) - *Savoir Scientifique et Pouvoir Social: L'École Polytechnique*. 1794-1914. Paris: Presses de la Fondation National des Sciences Politiques. p. 141.

economic backgrounds and generally distanced the working classes from the university. In 1860, tuition fees amounted to 26,400 *réis* per year[38], roughly corresponding to one month's salary for a university teacher. This explains why the lower classes were left out. Their presence at Coimbra would have been due to unquestionable personal merit, favourable logistical conditions (such as already living in the city of Coimbra), as well as financial support.

In fact, the growth in the number of schools and the relative widening of access to the university came along with the formalisation of certain means of economic support available to students from modest backgrounds. In theory at least, these were designed to curb the elitist structure of the higher education system. It was in this context that the Philanthropic-Academic Society (Sociedade Filantrópica-Académica) was founded in 1862. This charitable institution was designed to help 'underprivileged academics' by subsidising their allowances and enrolment fees, or just their enrolment fees[39]. Little research done on the social conditions of these early scholarship holders makes it difficult to determine whether this or other types of financial support – provided by the university or other entities – mitigated the effects of the selective nature of the education[40]. However, it is safe to presume that social status was among

[38] The amount gained by adding the 'registration opening fee' to the 'registration closing fee' for the year 1861-1862: UCA, University of Coimbra, Administração e Contabilidade, Correspondência-ofícios do Reitor e da Repartição de Contabilidade. Livro de Registo. 1861-1867. fl.10v-11.

[39] Scholarships were created by the decree of 22 March 1911, replacing (with modifications) the Philanthropic Society in providing financial support to low-income students: Teixeira Bastos (1923) - *Iniciativas académicas I – Sociedade Filantrópica-Académica de Coimbra*. Coimbra: Imprensa da Universidade. p. 7-8.

[40] In 1808, some students from Casa Pia de Lisboa were 'assisted by the General Police Superintendence' (UCA. University of Coimbra. Registo de Ordens Régias 1794-1829. fl. 112v-113). Around 1860, the University provided financial support for some students, covering their tuition fees, books, and allowances (UCA. University of Coimbra. Administração e Contabilidade. Correspondência-ofícios do Reitor e da Repartição de Contabilidade. Livro de Registo. 1861- 1867. fl. 10v-11; 40v; 67v; 70; 82v-83; 101-101v).

the criteria for the attribution of 'scholarships', and that the working classes, or petite bourgeoisie, were, in fact, the greatest benefactors. Given the above, the question arises as to whether the University of Coimbra was a place of legitimation for the upper classes. There is no doubt, though, that the institution provided a path for social mobility, rendering those who became associated with it a sense of belonging to an elite that was recognisable throughout Portugal.

In turn, a study of the geographical region of origin of the students helps to establish the university's sphere of influence, as well as to characterise the academic youth with greater precision. The data presented paints the University of Coimbra as a regional institution, with most of its students flocking from northern and central Portugal (see Table 6). The Tagus River borders the area to the south, with the University's influence registering as practically insignificant in the districts of Portalegre, Beja, Évora, and Faro over all the periods under analysis. An uneven distribution of students can be registered throughout Portugal, with students coming mainly from the districts of Coimbra, Porto, Viseu, and Lisbon, which together account for more than 40 per cent of the university's students throughout the nineteenth century: 49.9 per cent in 1836-37; 49 per cent in 1861-62; and 43.8 per cent in 1909-10. This shows no substantial differences with the distribution arrived at by Fernando Taveira da Fonseca for Canon Law and Law graduates between 1700 and 1770[41]. These students also originated from the central and northern regions of Portugal, particularly from the coastal strip between Minho and Setúbal. This distribution is echoed in research by Rui Cascão and Maria Manuel Almeida for the entirety of students in the years 1891-1900[42]. The geographical recruitment

[41] Fernando Taveira da Fonseca (1995) - *A Universidade de Coimbra (1700-1771). Estudo social e económico*. Coimbra: Por ordem da Universidade. p. 159-92.

[42] Rui Cascão and Maria Manuel Almeida (1991) - "Origens sociais dos alunos matriculados na Universidade de Coimbra nos finais do século XIX". In *Universidade(s),*

is thus demonstrated to have been remarkable over time, although slight changes can be noted from one district to another.

Though prior to 1909-10 most of the University's students came from the district of Coimbra, that academic year was a turning point, after which a more diverse spread of students was registered. Judging by the absolute and relative or density values (that is, the number of students per 1,000 inhabitants), students generally came from all over Portugal, with no particular district standing out as having supplied more students. Student density was low, with no significant differences between districts, due to numbers being relatively balanced. However, Coimbra remained well ahead. Geographical proximity favoured local enrolment within the district, specifically of students born in the City of Coimbra itself, who accounted for half of the district's student body (45 per cent). There were few students from the Portuguese islands of the Azores and Madeira. The University's ability to attract students from outside Portugal was limited, reaching only the Portuguese empire and colonies, as well as areas of significant Portuguese emigration, with Brazil being the only, yet modest, exception.

Table 6. Geographical origins of first-year students

	1780-81		**1836-37**		**1861-62**		**1909-10**		**Total**	
	Nr.	%	Nr.	%	Nr.	%	Nr.	%	Nr.	%
Aveiro	11	3.78	23	10.8	16	6.37	23	4.48	73	5.76
Beja	5	1.72	1	0.47	5	1.99	4	0.78	15	1.18
Braga	4	1.37	12	5.63	13	5.18	45	8.77	74	5.84
Bragança	3	1.03	8	3.76	14	5.58	8	1.56	33	2.60
Castelo Branco	4	1.37	5	2.35	13	5.18	26	5.07	48	3.79
Coimbra	21	7.22	54	25.40	53	21.10	80	15.60	208	16.40
Évora	3	1.03	3	1.41	5	1.99	11	2.14	22	1.74

História. Memória. Perspectivas, Congresso História da Universidade. vol. 3, Coimbra. p. 181-193.

Faro	2	0.69	1	0.47	4	1.59	18	3.51	25	1.97
Guarda	4	1.37	6	2.82	9	3.59	42	8.19	61	4.81
Leiria	8	2.75	3	1.41	4	1.59	6	1.17	21	1.66
Lisbon	22	7.56	14	6.57	22	8.76	42	8.19	100	7.89
Portalegre	8	2.75	3	1.41	5	1.99	12	2.34	28	2.21
Porto	15	5.15	27	12.70	13	5.18	64	12.50	119	9.38
Santarém	4	1.37	11	5.16	13	5.18	18	3.51	46	3.63
Viana do Castelo	4	1.37	3	1.41	9	3.59	11	2.14	27	2.13
Vila Real	6	2.06	13	6.10	7	2.79	29	5.65	55	4.34
Viseu	24	8.25	11	5.16	34	13.50	39	7.70	108	8.52
Angra	-	-	1	0.47	1	0.40	3	0.58	5	0.39
Horta	-	-	2	0.94	3	1.20	4	0.78	9	0.71
Ponta Delgada	-	-	1	0.47	-	-	6	1.17	7	0.55
Funchal	1	0.34	3	1.41	-	-	7	1.36	11	0.87
Brazil	9	3.09	8	3.76	7	2.79	4	0.78	28	2.21
India	-	-	-	0	1	0.40	1	0.19	2	0.16
From beyond	2	0.69	1	0.47	-	-	8	1.56	11	0.87
Unspecified	133	45.70	-	-	-	-	2	0.39	143	11.30
Total	291	100	213	100	251	99.9	513	100	1268	100

Source: UCA, Age Certificates.

This rough sketch of the student population allows for some firmer lines to be drawn regarding the profile of the average Coimbra student. They pursued a law curriculum, as this would best prepare them for political life. They came from northern or central Portugal and belonged to the upper middle class. The group spirit was thus reinforced by common social parameters and geographical origin, to which other factors, such as the same age, contributed. Students began their higher studies relatively early, and there were no significant variations in the ages of students when they entered university over time. On average, age ranged from 18.8 years in 1780-81 to 20.4 years in 1909-10 (Table 7). A certain continuity can be traced in view of the above, although student ages did rise slightly. This is particularly with the case for theology students, whose age spectrum was broader, ranging from between 17 to 20.75 years. In any case, the two most notable age groups for each period under analysis are the same (14-18 years and 19-23 years). As such, the minimal percentages of younger students (under 14 years old) and older students (over 24 and especially over 29 years old) are irrelevant, as seen in Table 8.

Table 7. The average age of students at university enrolment

	1780-81	**1836-37**	**1861-62**	**1909-10**
University (overall)	18.80	19.50	20.70	20.40
School of Law	19.21	19.78	19.63	20.51
School of Philosophy	17.90	–	16.25	20.00
School of Mathematics	20.92	19.02	19.50	19.49
School of Medicine	–	–	20.50	22.33
School of Theology	17.00	17.00	18.60	20.75
School of Mathematics / Philosophy	–	–	–	21.50
School of Pharmacy	–	–	–	21.29

Source: UCA., Age Certificates.

Table 8. Age of students at university enrolment by age bracket

	1780-81		**1836-37**		**1861-62**		**1909-10**	
Age bracket	Nr.	%	Nr.	%	Nr.	%	Nr.	%
< 14	4	1.4	–	–	–	–	–	–
14–18	70	24	74	35	74	29	144	28
19–23	46	16	90	42	108	43	301	58
24–28	9	3.1	12	5.6	23	9.2	57	11
> 28	3	1	2	0.9	15	6	6	1.2
Unspecified	161	55	36	17	31	12	13	2.5
Total	293	100	214	100	251	100	521	100

Source: UCA., Age Certificates.

3. Aspects of everyday life

> [...] I put on my gown, [and] bought furniture, which consisted of a bedstead, a mattress, a chair, a pine bench, and a bookshelf. I put the same servant in charge of the household, and my cohort sent me to the College of Arts to take the so-called courtyard ("pátio") exams, without which no one could enrol at the university, except as a listener[43].

Upon arrival in Coimbra, any student's main concern would have been to find accommodation. Faced with a pressing need for somewhere to live, students would look for a house or room, often basing their choice on distance from the university as well as the cost of rent. Most students lived in the Bairro Alto, the neighbourhood surrounding the university. This area was, however, slowly depopulated of its academic population in the second half of the nineteenth century as students spread out to other urban areas. This can be clearly seen in the fact that 68 per cent of first-year students living on the university hill in 1861-62, compared with only 43 per cent of freshmen in 1909-10 (Table 9)[44]. The disrepair of properties, the urban renewal of the city, and the improvements in public transport were the most likely factors influencing residential choice away from traditional locations. In fact, an expansion

---

[43] Translated from Guilherme Centazzi (1840) - *O estudante de Coimbra ou relampago da historia portugueza desde 1826 ate 1838*. vol. 1, Lisbon: Typographia de Antonio Jose da Rocha. p. 32-33.

[44] In the late nineteenth century, a 'novice' was a first-year student in any school except Medicine, as these students had already concluded their preparatory studies in Philosophy and Mathematics. 'Freshmen' (*caloiros*) were students in their final year of secondary school or prep students. While these two terms were synonymous in the first decade of the twentieth century, the former seems to have disappeared, resulting in only the term *caloiro* being used: Amílcar Ferreira de Castro (1947) - *A gíria dos estudantes de Coimbra*. Coimbra: FLUC. p. 56-58, 89; Maria Eduarda Cruzeiro (1979) -"Costumes estudantis estudantis no século XIX: tradição e conservação institucional". *Análise Social*. XV. p. 798; Manuel Alberto Carvalho Prata - *A Academia de Coimbra..., ob. cit.*,. vol. 1, nr. 796. p. 361.

of the housing market in Coimbra was registered from the third quarter of the nineteenth century onwards, thanks to new areas being integrated into the urban fabric, to street improvements, and the building of new neighbourhoods[45].

Table 9. Location of first-year student accommodation in Coimbra

	1861-62		**1909-10**	
	Nr.	%	Nr.	%
Alta	171	68.1	225	43.2
Baixa	34	13.5	25	4.8
Other areas	23	9.2	108	20.7
Unspecified	23	9.2	163	31.3
Total	251	100	521	100

Sources: UCA, Student List (1862), Yearbook (1910), José Pinto Loureiro (1960-1964) - *Toponímia de Coimbra*, 2 vols. Coimbra.

Other obstacles had to be overcome, the main one being the resistance of property owners who were opposed to student renting, given the problems that would inevitably arise with neighbours, especially if they knew or suspected that their house was going to become a fraternity (the so-called *república*)[46]. Once this obstacle had been overcome, the type of accommodation selected depended on each individual's economic circumstances and the allowance provided by their parents[47]. There is little information available

[45] Armando Carneiro da Silva (1967) - "Evolução populacional coimbrã". Separata de *Arquivo Coimbrão*, XXIII. 1968; João Lourenço Roque (1991) - "Coimbra na 2ª metade do Século XIX. Estudantes e sociabilidade urbana (alguns aspectos)". In *Universidade(s), História. Memória. Perspectivas, Congresso História da Universidade* - vol. 3, Coimbra. p. 258.

[46] Prata. *A Academia de Coimbra*. vol. 1. p. 338.

[47] Student demonstrations were not limited to those relating to politics or the institution. Protests against the urban population were also frequent, especially due to the high prices charged by landlords for accommodation. The stand taken by the students ('Tomarada') in 1854, when, armed, they left Coimbra in protest, can be

on the cost of rents, although some data is occasionally found. It is known, for example, that properties owned by the university were leased to students. Rents for houses on the 'lower level of the Liceu' in around the year 1855 ranged from 9,690 to 12,100 *réis* a year and were collected in Michaelmas[48]. Memoirs are filled with references to decrepit dwellings[49], to truly modest rooms, and to fraternities[50]. As stated by José Lobo d'Ávila Lima, in our translation, the most common way of living in Coimbra was 'as a fraternity [...] Three, four, even six people (over half a dozen was a couple of steps short of anarchy) would rent a house, pay for it [...] and in return for 10 or 12 thousand *réis* a month, they were settled'[51]. Exceptionally, if a student were on a full allowance, they would take residence at a hotel in the city, as was the case of first-year law student Manuel Frota Vieira de Mascarenhas in 1909-10, who was born in Santa Comba Dão and whose father was an administrative judge. 'Feudal opulence' characterised Macedo Papança, the Count of Monsaraz, who lived in a house with forty-two rooms, switching bedroom every other day[52].

In addition to accommodation expenses, students would also have to cover the cost of furniture, food, and their servants' wages, or 'the old women serving the students', as Guilherme Centazzi

---

seen as symptomatic. Tempers then calmed in Tomar thanks to negotiations with the authorities: Luís Reis Torgal (1993) - "A instrução pública", *História de Portugal*. vol. 5, Lisbon. p. 637.

[48] UCA, University of Coimbra, Administração e Contabilidade. Receita e despesa. Contas da receita e despesa, 1849-1885, fl. 2v; 4v; 5v.

[49] Alberto Costa (known as Ex-Pad Zé) (1951) - *O Livro do Doutor Assis*. Lisbon. p. 42.

[50] Alberto Sousa Lamy (1990) - *A Academia de Coimbra 1537-1990. História, praxe, boémia e estudo, partidas e piadas, organismos académicos*. Lisboa: Rei dos Livros. p. 708-10; Manuel Alberto Carvalho Prata - *A Academia de Coimbra..., ob. cit.*,. vol. 1. p. 340-352.

[51] José Lobo d´Ávila Lima - "Meio seculo de vida coimbrã". *Illustração Portugueza*. 2nd series (23 July 1906). p. 690.

[52] *Idem, Ibidem*. p. 688.

called them[53]. While no information is available on the individuals themselves, the wage paid would have depended on the quality and quantity of the help hired, which would generally have been modest[54]. Sources tell us that around 1830 wages varied between 480 and 600 *réis* per month[55], and had increased by the end of the century. Books, or more specifically notebooks[56], as well as tuition fees, were also among the expenses that every university student had to pay.

It is generally difficult to accurately estimate the average cost of living in Coimbra. Naturally, this would have varied over time. However, an attempt can be made by referring to the expenses of some students who were subsidised by the university in 1861 and 1862. These were registered at around 140,000 *réis* per year, which would have covered the tuition fee, books, and a living allowance[57]. The monthly amount for the latter (12,000 *réis*) is similar to that noted by Trindade Coelho (n.d., 133) as a standard university student allowance, placed at 10,000 *réis* (students with allowances of more than 30,000 *réis* were considered rich). This figure is close to the monthly fees charged at some of the country's most prestigious schools for both boys and girls[58], serving as proof of the educational

[53] Guilherme Centazzi - *O estudante de Coimbra... ob. cit.*. p. 32.

[54] Manuel Alberto Carvalho Prata - *A Academia de Coimbra..., ob. cit.,*. vol. 1. p.. 345-47.

[55] Guilherme Centazzi - *O estudante de Coimbra... ob. cit.*. p. 32.

[56] According to Trindade Coelho, 'there weren't even books, because the lecturers did not care to make them, and that was why we needed notebooks', which cost around 350 *réis* in 1870: *In Illo tempore (s. d.).* Lisbon: Europa-América. p. 107, 134.

[57] This is the case for law student José Correia Loureiro, who, in 1861, received 137,900 *réis* from the university, as follows: tuition fees for enrollment (13,200 *réis*), books for the year (3,500 *réis*), monthly allowances for the months of October 1861 to June 1862 at 12,000 *réis* per month (108,000 *réis*), and enrolment closing fee at the end of the academic year (13,200 *réis*): UCA, University of Coimbra. Administração e Contabilidade. Correspondência. Ofícios do Reitor e da Repartição de Contabilidade. Livro de Registo 1861-1867, fl. 10v-11.

[58] The monthly fee for students at S. Fiel School in Louriçal do Campo was 8,000 *réis* in around 1880: Joaquim Augusto de Sousa Refoios (1883) - *O Collegio de S. Fiel no Louriçal do Campo e o de Nossa Senhora da Conceição na Covilhã. Apontamentos*

establishment's social selectivity. In fact, only wealthy families could cover the costs associated with living in the City of Coimbra. The time spent there, however, was a learning experience: 'In Coimbra, isolated, far from their families [...] the freshmen would unwind and let their hair down. Aware of the limits of their allowance, they would sweep away the dark dust of prejudice, often feeling the depths of necessity', as José Lobo d'Ávila Lima wrote[59]. As a rule, the allowance was advanced by the city's merchants, to whom the students were "recommended". This, together with the high cost of renting rooms, was one of the main reasons for the youth protests against the "futricas", and the cause of many conflicts or disturbances between students and the urban working class, such as the "Tomarada" in February 1854[60].

Once the issue of accommodation had been solved and some formalities completed (namely, filing the preparatory exam certificates, obtaining the rector's authorisation, and registering as a student), 'novices' could start attending classes. A common practice was to mock the freshmen ('cassoar os caloiros'). Judging from some testimonies, this came under substantial criticism by certain students. One such student was Francisco Soares Franco, who plainly stated: 'It is a bitter mockery of common sense, which has been passed down from generation to generation. The ruthless reception of the wretched is a poignant insult to reason', adding that 'the madness ingrained by barbaric custom gives rise to neither remorse among the executioners, nor resentment among the victims. They were freshmen. No further

sobre o Jesuitismo no districto de Castello Branco. Coimbra: Imprensa da Universidade. p. 24. The monthly fee for Ursulinas School in Coimbra reached 10,000 *réis* in the 1870s: Irene Maria Vaquinhas (1996-1997) - "Alguns aspectos da vida quotidiana num colégio feminino do século XIX: o caso do Real Colégio Ursulino das Chagas de Coimbra (1874-1880)". In *Gestão e desenvolvimento*. V.VI. p. 218.

[59] José Lobo d´Ávila Lima - "Meio seculo de vida coimbrã...", *art. cit.*. p. 690.

[60] *O Conimbricense* 11, 14 e 23 de Fevereiro de 1854.

explanation is necessary'[61]. The practices of the University in the 19th century are well-known through the works of Maria Eduarda Cruzeiro, particularly concerning the teaching practices developed, the schedules followed, and the assessment methods used[62]. By the Pombaline reform, students were required to attend classes, as well as what they called 'the lesson' (*sabatina*, a review of the week's classwork), among other school requirements. Memoirs provide detailed accounts of the strategies employed as well as the ruses devised by students to evade the attendance rules and escape interrogation.

Conclusion

The University of Coimbra was an intellectual and academic centre of reputed importance, having educated a considerable number of those who went on to occupy important positions in Portuguese society. These included public and private, civil, military, and religious positions in both science and the arts. The expected post-university trajectory explains the significant, though irregular, influx of students to the university in certain periods within the chronological framework considered, and even the breadth of its geographical area of influence. An observation of the data confirms this idea, considering that people of various backgrounds from all over Portugal studied there, although it is worth noting the predominance of students from the centre of the country, particularly from the district of Coimbra itself. It should be noted, however, that an exact quantification is difficult. Naturally, there are discrepancies in the numbers and statistics obtained by various authors, which

---

[61] Francisco Soares Franco (1867) - *Memorias da mocidade. As rosas e os espinhos do amor*. Lisbon. p. 45.

[62] Maria Eduarda Cruzeiro - *Action symbolique et formation scolaire ... ob. cit.*. tome 1. p. 263-289.

are justified by certain ambiguities. In many cases, the difficulty in objectively specifying the social background of students has been made clear. This is often due to this information not being registered or being poorly defined. In addition to the frequent omission of this information, the data provided are often dubious and ambiguous.

Despite the attractiveness of the University of Coimbra, there is no denying its classist structure, with students from the middle and upper classes predominant, compared toa small number of students from less wealthy backgrounds. The concept of 'bourgeoisness' was therefore intrinsic to this context, having become increasingly ingrained from the mid-nineteenth century onwards. In fact, bourgeois norms were born precisely in the context of new concerns surrounding economic profit and new socio-political landscapes. In other words, an urgent need arose among the bourgeoisie to turn away from clerical tutelage in teaching, replacing these teachings with those of a bourgeois nature that would better serve their interests. In practice, this meant training men to operate in a liberal state. Nineteenth-century university students were no longer clerics or nobles; rather, they were the sons of the emerging bourgeoisie who needed higher education as a means of entering society as professionals, while members of the petite bourgeoisie and lower classes were left behind. A fundamental goal was made clear: educating an elite that would firstly propagate liberal ideologies, and secondly their scientific abilities. It is therefore unsurprising that the School of Law was the largest in terms of student numbers, it being the most influential and the source of the guiding principles required in the nineteenth century – the consummate century of administration, despite the urgency of training the technicians necessary to overhaul the Portuguese economy.

As regards the student's daily life, it was largely filled with routines, habits and customs, many of which already rooted in tradition. Our focus is on these actors and their concerns, not only as agents of university life but also as active participants in the life of the city. Without going into further detail about academic life, from the data gathered and the research carried out on the actions taken and interactions experienced, it can be concluded that the reference group, the students have had a highly relevant and multifaceted experience. Within this context, a closer look at the individual portraits of the students, as reflected in their memoirs, reveals the main elements contributing to their daily lives. Students formed a tightly-knit group, set apart by the expression of their claims, as well as feelings, the evidence for their practices, their self-representation, and the specificity of the linguistic and symbolic forms which they chose to employ. In short, the interaction between the University and public life, and the interconnections between citizens and politics, were mirrored in the close connections between the university and urban life. Life in the city of Coimbra in other times, both past and future, can be concluded to have revolved around the university.

Sources and Bibliography

Manuscript sources

University of Coimbra Archive (UCA)

Certidões de Idade, Actos e Graus (1785-1788);

Certidões de Idade (2ª série) 1834-1900;

Certidões de Idade (1909-1910);

Livros de Matrículas (1909-1910);

Universidade de Coimbra, Administração e Contabilidade, Correspondência-ofícios do Reitor e da Repartição de Contabilidade, Livro de Registo, 1861-1867;

Exames (1772-1773 a 1789-1790);

Actos Grandes e Graus de Doutor (1772-1784);

Processos e inscrição (1909-1910)

Livros de Matrículas (1909-1910)

Processos de cartas de curso (SR), 3.ª série, cx. 68 (Farmácia, 1869).

Bibliography

Annuario da Universidade de Coimbra, Anno Lectivo de 1909-1910 (1910). Coimbra: Imprensa da Universidade; https://digitalis-dsp.uc.pt/republica/UCBG-8-118-1-3/UCBG-8-118-2-1909-1910/UCBG-8-118-2-1909-1910_item2/UCBG-8-118-2-1909-1910_PDF/UCBG-8-118-2-1909-1910_PDF_24-C-R0120/UCBG-8-118-2-1909-1910_0000_Obra_Completa_t24-C-R0120.pdf

Baldó i Lacomba, Marc (1984). *Profesores y estudiantes en la epoca romantica. La Universidad de Valencia en la crisis del Antiguo Regimen (1786-1843)*. Valencia: Ayuntamiento de Valencia.

Bandeira, Ana Maria Leitão; Pita, João Rui Rocha (1990), "As primeiras mulheres farmacêuticas na Universidade de Coimbra". *Kalliope. De medicina*. nº3. 21-28.

Bastos, Teixeira (1923) - *Iniciativas académicas I – Sociedade Filantrópica – Académica de Coimbra*, Coimbra: Imprensa da Universidade.

Boavida, Ana Maria Caiado (1983) - "Tópicos sobre a prática política dos estudantes republicanos, 1890-1931: limites e condicionalismos do movimento estudantil", *Análise Social*, nº19 (77-78-79), 1983, pp. 743-756; http://analisesocial.ics.ul.pt/documentos/1245161185S5qCW6mr1Qg90EC2.pdf.

Burney, John M. (1988) -*Toulouse et son université. Facultés et étudiants dans la France provinciale du 19e siècle*. Toulouse: Éditions du Centre National de la Recherche Scientifique-Presses Universitaires du Mirail.

Caron, Jean-Claude (1991) - *Générations romantiques. Les étudiantes de Paris et le Quartier Latin (1814-1851)*. Paris: Armand Colin.

Carvalho, Ana Marcella de (2019) - *As mulheres na Universidade de Coimbra ao tempo da Primeira República (1910-1926)*. Coimbra: FLUC (Master's dissertation), http://hdl.handle.net/10316/86399.

Cascão, Rui (1993) - "Demografia e sociedade". *História de Portugal*, vol. V, *O Liberalismo*. Direção de José Mattoso. Lisboa: Editorial Estampa. p. 425-439.

Cascão, Rui e Almeida, Maria Manuel (1991) - "Origens sociais dos alunos matriculados na Universidade de Coimbra nos finais do século XIX", *Universidade (s), História. Memória. Perspectivas, Congresso História da Universidade*, 7° Centenário, Actas, vol. 3, Coimbra. p. 181-193.

Castro, Amílcar Ferreira de (1947) - *A gíria dos estudantes de Coimbra*, Coimbra: Faculdade de Letras.

Centazzi, Guilherme (1840) - *O estudante de Coimbra ou relampago da historia portugueza desde 1826 ate 1838*, tomo 1°, Lisboa: Typographia de Antonio Jose da Rocha.

Coelho, Trindade (s.d.) - *In Illo tempore*, Lisboa: Livros de Bolso Europa-América

Costa, Alberto (Ex-Pad Zé) (1951) - *O Livro do Doutor Assis*, 10ª edição, Lisboa: Livraria Clássica Editora & Cª..

Cruz, Maria Antonieta (1994) - *Os burgueses do Porto na segunda metade do século XIX*. Porto: Faculdade de Letras da Universidade do Porto (PhD thesis), 3 vols.

Cruzeiro, Maria Eduarda (1990) - *Action symbolique et formation scolaire. L' Université de Coimbra et sa Faculté de Droit dans la seconde moitié du XIXᵉ siècle*. Tomes 1 et 2. Paris. (PhD thesis).

Cruzeiro, Maria Eduarda (1988) - "A reforma pombalina na história da Universidade", *Análise Social*, vol. XXIV (100), 1988 (1°), p. 165-210; http://analisesocial.ics.ul.pt/documentos/1223029550B7xEB9pj4Ht43DJ4.pdf.

Cruzeiro, Maria Eduarda (1979) - "Costumes estudantis no século XIX: tradição e conservação institucional", *Análise Social*, vol. XV (60), 1979-4ª, p. 795-838, http://analisesocial.ics.ul.pt/documentos/1223990403T2oCN9gi5Xo15HK9.pdf.

Ferreira, António Aurélio da Costa (1915) - *Noutros Tempos*. Coimbra: Livraria Neves Êditora.

Ferreira, Fátima Moura (2010) - "Os juristas e a representação política", *Respublica. Cidadania e representação política em Portugal 1820-1926*, Catroga, Fernando; Almeida, Pedro Tavares de (Coord.). Lisboa: Assembleia da República / Biblioteca Nacional de Portugal. p. 216-229.

Fonseca, Cardoso (1911) - *Outros tempos ou velharias de Coimbra 1850 a 1880*, Lisboa: Livraria Tabuense.

Fonseca, Fernando Taveira da (1995) - *A Universidade de Coimbra (1700-1771) (Estudo social e económico)*. Coimbra: Por Ordem da Universidade.

Franco, Francisco Soares (1867) - *Memorias da mocidade. As rosas e os espinhos do amor*. Lisbon.

Frijhoff, William (1986) - "Grandeur des nombres et misères des realités: la courbe de Franz Eulenburg et le débat sur le nombre d' intellectuels en Allemagne, 1576-1815". In *Les universités européennes du XVIe au XVIIIe siècle. Histoire sociale des populations* étudiantes. Tome I. Études rassemblés par Dominique Julia, Jacques Revel, Roger Chartier. Paris: Éditions de l'École des Hautes Études en Sciences Sociales. p. 23-63.

Gomes, Joaquim Ferreira (1987) - *A mulher na Universidade de Coimbra*. Coimbra: Livraria Almedina.

Gomes, Joaquim Ferreira (1986) - "As primeiras mulheres que frequentaram a Universidade de Coimbra (1891-1910)". *Boletim do Arquivo da Universidade de Coimbra*, vol. VIII. p. 243-257.

Lamy, Alberto Sousa (1990) - *A Academia de Coimbra 1537-1990. História, praxe, boémia e estudo, partidas e piadas, organismos académicos*. Lisboa: Rei dos Livros.

Legislação academica colligida pelo Dr. José Maria de Abreu. Coordenada, revista e ampliada pelo Dr. António dos Santos Viegas, vol. I, 1772-1850 (1894). Coimbra: Imprensa da Universidade.

Lima, José Lobo d´Ávila (23 July 1906) - "Meio seculo de vida coimbrã". *Illustração Portugueza*. 2nd series. p. 685-695.

Loureiro, José Pinto (1960-1964) - *Toponímia de Coimbra*, 2 tomos, Coimbra: Edição da Câmara Municipal.

Madeira, António Carneiro dos Santos (s. d) - *A Universidade de Coimbra no século XIX (Matrículas das várias faculdades no ano letivo de 1861-1862)*. Coimbra: FLUC (academic work).

Memoria Professorum Universitatis Conimbrigensis. 1772-1937 (1992). vol. II. Dir. Manuel Augusto Rodrigues. Coimbra: Arquivo da Universidade de Coimbra.

Peset, Mariano; Peset, Jose Luis (1974) - *La Universidad Española (Siglos XVIII y XIX). Despotismo Ilustrado y Revolucion Liberal.* Madrid: Taurus Ediciones, S. A..

Prata, Manuel Alberto Carvalho (1994) - *A Academia de Coimbra (1880-1926). Sociedade, cultura e política.* 2 vols. Coimbra: s. n. (PhD thesis).

Prost, Antoine (1968) - *L'enseignement en France 1800-1967.* Paris: Armand Colin.

Refoios, Joaquim Augusto de Sousa (1883) - *O Collegio de S. Fiel no Louriçal do Campo e o de Nossa Senhora da Conceição na Covilhã. Apontamentos sobre o Jesuitismo no districto de Castello Branco*, Coimbra: Imprensa da Universidade.

Regulamento para a fiscalização e julgamento das faltas dos estudantes da Universidade de Coimbra (1904). Coimbra: Imprensa da Universidade.

Reis, Carlos Xavier (2023) – *A Universidade de Coimbra e os seus estudantes. Aos olhos dos viajantes estrangeiros (1581-1879).* Coimbra: Imprensa da Universidade.

Relação e indice alphabetico dos estudantes matriculados na Universidade de Coimbra no anno lectivo de 1836 para 1837, suas naturalidades, filiações e moradas (1836). Coimbra: na Imprensa da Universidade.

Relação e indice alphabetico dos estudantes matriculados na Universidade de Coimbra no Anno lectivo de 1861 para 1862, com suas filiações, naturalidades e moradas e a designação das diversas cadeiras e disciplinas, e dos lentes e professores respectivos (1862). Coimbra: na Imprensa da Universidade.

Roque, João Lourenço (1991) - "Coimbra na 2ª metade do Século XIX. Estudantes e sociabilidade urbana (alguns aspectos)". In *Universidade(s), História. Memória. Perspectivas, Congresso História da Universidade.* vol. 3, Coimbra, 1991. p. 257-275.

Simone, Maria Rosa di (1996) - "A admissão". In Ruëgg, Walter (Coordenação). *Uma história da Universidade na Europa.* Vol. II. *As Universidades na Europa Moderna (1500-1800)*, Coordenadora da edição Hilde de Ridder-Symoens. Lisboa: Conselho de Reitores das Universidades Portuguesas / Fundação Eng. António de Almeida / Imprensa Nacional Casa da Moeda. p. 277-313.

Shinn, Terry (1980) - *Savoir Scientifique et Pouvoir Social: L'École Polytechnique. 1794-1914.* Paris: Presses de la Fondation National des Sciences Politiques.

Silva, Armando Carneiro da (1967) - "Evolução populacional coimbrã", separata do *Arquivo Coimbrão*, vol. XXIII, Coimbra.

Torgal, Luís Reis (2013) - "Universidade de Coimbra". In *Dicionário de História da I República e do Republicanismo.* vol. III: N-Z. Lisboa: Edição Assembleia da República – Divisão de Edições. p. 1053-1060.

Torgal, Luís Reis (1990) - "A instrução pública". In *História de Portugal*, vol. V, Lisboa: Círculo de Leitores. p. 609-651.

Torgal, Luís Reis (1990 A) - "A Universidade de Coimbra entre o dinamismo e o estrangulamento cultural". In *Portugal Contemporâneo*, dir. de António Reis. vol. II, Lisboa: Publicações Alfa. p. 257-262.

Torgal, Luís Reis (1990) - "Universidade, conservadorismo e dinâmica de mudança nos primórdios do liberalismo em Portugal". *Revista de História das Ideias*, nº12. Coimbra. p. 129-219.

Torgal, Luís Reis (1987) - "Passos Manuel e a Universidade. Do Vintismo ao Setembrismo". *Cultura, História e Filosofia*, 6, Lisboa. p. 79-92.

Torremocha Hernández, Margarita (1995) - "La población estudiantil de la Universidad de Oñate. Siglo XVII". In *Investigaciones Históricas*, nº 15. Universidad de Valladolid. p. 209-239.

Vaquinhas, Irene (2018) - "Mulheres na Universidade de Coimbra: o caso das primeiras estudantes cabo-verdianas" / "Women at the University of Coimbra: the case of the first Cape Verdean female students", *História. Revista da FLUP*. Porto. IV Série. Vol. 8, nº 1. p. 219-244. DOI: 1021747/0871164X/hist8a12.

Vaquinhas, Irene (1996-1997) - "Alguns aspectos da vida quotidiana num colégio feminino do século XIX: o caso do Real Colégio Ursulino das Chagas de Coimbra (1874-1880). In *Gestão e desenvolvimento*, nº5-6, Viseu, Universidade Católica Portuguesa. p. 213-247, http://hdl.handle.net/10316/33121.

Vasconcelos, António de (1941) - "Estatística dos estudantes matriculados na Universidade de Coimbra durante o século XIX, e dos graus de licenciado e de doutor nela conferidos no mesmo século, isto é, desde 1 de Janeiro de 1801 até 31 de Dezembro de 1900". *Escritos Vários*. vol. II. Coimbra: Coimbra Editora Lda., p. 124-140.

Gender and politics at the University of Coimbra, Portugal: the case of Aurora, a rebellious student, 1915-1916

Irene Vaquinhas
https://orcid.org/0000-0003-1889-165X

Abstract

In 1916, Aurora Teixeira de Castro, a student at the Faculty of Law of the University of Coimbra, on learning that she had failed an exam, questioned some members of the jury and challenged their decision. Her stance was supported by two fellow students who used aggressive language. As a result, a case was filed with the academic police against the students, which led to a movement in solidarity with the "victims" and in protest against the University of Coimbra.

An analysis of these proceedings provides a study of gender representations in higher education at a time when women were being admitted to university courses. The rebellious behaviour that surrounded the case, triggered by a person who belonged to the first generation of women to graduate in law in Portugal and who would become the first female notary in Europe, also signalled a break with the traditional female archetype associated with submission and passivity, and reflected changes in gender identities and challenges to the symbols of power under the democratic First Republic.

Keywords

University of Coimbra / Portugal; Proceedings of the Academic Police; First Republic; Aurora Teixeira de Castro; Political opposition and student mobilisation; History of women and gender studies.

Introduction

At around midday on 26 July 1916, at the Faculty of Law of the University of Coimbra, Aurora Teixeira de Castro (1891-1938), a student in her fourth year, 25 years old and married, began to question Dr. António Faria de Carneiro Pacheco, after learning that she had failed the state exam in Economic and Political Sciences (Additional Paper). This law professor was one of the four members of the jury who walked down the Via Latina stairs. She asked about the authority behind the proposed failure, supported by her fellow student and husband, Jaime Cardoso de Gouveia. The latter, angrily, declared that it was "cowardice to fail a lady", and shouted "I would like to see you gentlemen use the proper criteria to fail students". His words were followed by insults such as "rogues and bandits"[1]. Another law student, Fernando Araújo, also intervened in the dispute and, brandishing his carved seahorse cane, added to the insults by proclaiming "this is despicable: cowards, villains, scoundrels, dogs, swindlers". Spurred on by his colleague Aurora, who complained "there goes that coward, running away", he ran across the courtyard after Dr. Domingos Fezas Vital, another member of the jury, shouting,

[1] University of Coimbra Archive (UCA), Processos de Polícia Académica (1916).

"Don't run off. Wait here, you cad". Faced with this intimidation, reinforced by the threatening gesture of the cane being waved in the air, the professor turned around and drew a pistol, "which he primed, but did not aim at his aggressor". The dispute was brought to an end by the prompt intervention of staff and students. They apprehended the student and escorted him out of the courtyard. Two days later, the "student republican newspaper" *A Revolta*, of which Fernando de Araújo was one of the editors, reported on the incident. The articles published were highly critical of the Faculty of Law, in particular, and the University of Coimbra in general[2].

After the case had been summarily reconstructed on the basis of witness statements, the academic police were immediately instructed by the Rector to open an inquiry into the "lack of respect" for the members of the jury, an act of disobedience covered by the University of Coimbra Academic Police Regulations of 25 November 1839[3], abolished during the First Republic but reintroduced for disciplinary purposes by Decree Nº. 197 of 22 August 1911[4]. Manuel Paulo Merêa[5], a law professor, was appointed prosecutor and would be responsible for handling the case, leading the inquiries and establishing the facts.

By providing an opportunity to challenge the university as an institution, the dispute set in motion by the student Aurora de Castro Gouveia became the starting point for a political and ideological reconfiguration of the event, spearheaded by the radical republican propaganda press. However, it is worth giving a brief overview of

---

[2] *A Revolta*, Ano 4º, nº 88, 29 Jul. 1916; UCA, Processos de Polícia Académica (1916).

[3] *Legislação Academica coligida pelo Dr. José Maria de Abreu e Coordenada, revista e ampliada pelo Dr. Antonio dos Santos Viegas*, vol. I, 1772-1850 (1894). Coimbra: Imprensa da Universidade; Título I, artº. 2. p. 223.

[4] "Penas disciplinares para os alunos dos institutos de ensino dependentes da Direcção Geral da Instrucção Secundária, Superior e Especial", Diário do Govêrno. 24 Aug. 1911. In *Anuário da Universidade de Coimbra*. Ano lectivo de 1911-1912, Coimbra: Imprensa da Universidade, 1912. p. 148-149.

[5] "Merêa, Manuel Paulo". *Memoria Professorum Universitatis Conimbrigensis. 1772-1937* (1992), vol. 2, Coimbra: Arquivo da Universidade de Coimbra. p. 161.

the University of Coimbra. It dates back to the 13th century and was organised on the basis of monastic schools, following the example of the oldest European universities (Bologna, Paris, Oxford, Salamanca, among others), with the studies in canon law being dominant[6]. Between that century and the 16th century, its location changed between Lisbon and Coimbra, until 1537, when it finally settled in Coimbra, remaining the only university in Portugal until the beginning of the 20th century. In the 18th century, it underwent a major reform that projected it externally, both on the continent and in the colonies (especially Brazil), contributing to the consolidation of a common cultural space and being one of the institutions responsible for ensuring the maintenance of the ruling classes and the political and administrative establishment. Since the beginning of the 19th century, first with the Liberal revolution (1820) and then with the republican struggle, in the transition from the 19th to the 20th century, the University was subject to deep criticism (ecclesiastical past, corporatism, memory-based teaching, demand for greater autonomy), despite the fact that it was trying to align itself with the construction of a new state and a new social, economic and cultural organisation. With the proclamation of the Republic on 5 October 1910, which put an end to the monarchical regime, the university system underwent significant changes. Coimbra´s monopoly on higher education came to an end with the creation of universities in Lisbon and Porto. The university structure was secularised, religious oaths were banned, and progress was made towards more experimental and scientific teaching[7].

[6] José Mattoso (1997) - "A universidade portuguesa e as universidades europeias". In *História da Universidade em Portugal*. I vol. (1290-1536). Universidade de Coimbra / Fundação Calouste Gulbenkian. p. 3-29.

[7] Maria Cândida Proença (2013) - "Ensino". In *Dicionário de História da I República e do Republicanismo*, vol. I: A-E. Lisbon: Assembleia da República. p. 1146. Since 2013 the architectural ensemble consisting of the University of Coimbra, Alta, and Sofia, has been considered a UNESCO World Heritage Site.

This act of defiance took place at a time when the university system was transitioning from a monarchical to a republican regime, in a context of great national economic, social and political instability, aggravated by military coups against the recently republican regime and the outbreak of the Great War[8]. During this period the student youth were not immune to the general context, with the main urban centres showing signs of agitation that affected various educational institutions, both higher and secondary and technical. In the city of Coimbra itself, riots broke out at the secondary school and the Escola Normal Superior in 1916, while in the cities of Lisbon and Porto there were strikes and demonstrations at the Instituto Superior Técnico and the Medical School[9].

The leading role played by a woman makes this case unprecedented and unique. It´s the first time in the history of the University of Coimbra that a woman has challenged the institution by questioning a decision made by the teaching staff. Aurora was admitted to the University in 1912. She was the only female student to enrol in the Faculty of Law that year and the second ever to complete the course. How did a woman's private protest over a failing grade become a factor in the critique of the education system and the university itself? Could the failure of the student be interpreted as a form of anti-feminism or discrimination, "soft violence" or, in the words of Luis Bonino Méndez[10], "micromachismo", against women being admitted to law faculties and subsequently pursuing legal careers, on the grounds that men were the legitimate beneficiaries of this university education? As Ana Vicente mentions, "anti-feminism |...| uses various strategies to hinder the affirmation of women.

---

[8] João B. Serra (2009) - "A evolução política (1910-1917)". In *História da Primeira República Portuguesa*, Coord. Fernando Rosas; Maria Fernanda Rollo. Lisbon: Tinta da China. p. 117.

[9] *Gazeta de Coimbra*, 9, 16, 19, 25 Feb. and 15 Mar. 1916.

[10] Luis Bonino Méndez (1998) - *Micromachismos: La violencia invisible en la pareja*.

Forbidding, hindering, |...| ignoring |...| preventing, ridiculing, despising"[11]. At the time, the degree did not entitle women to any professional rights, as this would not be officially recognised until 1918 and 1919 for the practice of the professions of lawyer, assistant registrar and notary. Hence, at that time, female graduates could not compete in the labour market. However, the debate on equal professional opportunities for men and women had already been begun in the women's and/or feminist press and in liberal and/or republican circles, both in parliament and within freemasonry. In addition, in 1913, the first Portuguese woman to graduate in law, Regina Quintanilha, began working as an officially appointed lawyer at the Court of Boa Hora in Lisbon[12], all of which occurred before the aforementioned legislation was introduced.

These are some of the issues that this study aims to address. The methodology begins with an analysis of the proceedings involving the academic police, in order to contextualize the disciplinary offence and reconstruct this exercise in correctional policing, the academic careers of those involved and the forms of support that were mobilised. The academic police at the University of Coimbra played a role in enforcing discipline and preventing offences. In the opinion of many students and professors, it was anachronistic and inappropriate for the late 19th century.

Since the Middle Ages, the University of Coimbra, like other Iberian universities or those in Latin America under the Old Regime[13],

---

[11] Ana Vicente (2009) - "Antifeminismo. A resistência ao evidente". In *Dança dos Demónios*. Coord. António Marujo and José Eduardo Franco, Lisbon: Temas e Debates. p. 431-483.

[12] Joaquim Ferreira Gomes - "Regina Quintanilha – a primeira caloira de Direito". In *Estudos para a história da Universidade de Coimbra*, Coimbra, 1991. p. 65-66; "D. Regina Quintanilha. O seu aparecimento como advogada nos tribunaes de Lisboa". In *Occidente. Revista Illustrada de Portugal e do Estrangeiro*, XXXVI vol., 30 Nov. 1913, nº 1257, 0368; "Sra. D. Regina Quintanilha". In *Ilustração Portugueza*, II série, nº 405, 24 Nov 1913.

[13] Gustavo Hernández Sánchez (2017) - "El fuero académico em la Real Universidad de México y otras atribuciones de su rectos: 1597-1640". In *Cuadernos de Historia*

had its own private jurisdiction and court of law with powers to hear civil and criminal cases. This jurisdiction was abolished in 1834, following the Liberal Revolution[14], although the academic police survived, governed by regulations issued in 1839, which combined and adapted a number of old provisions[15]. The police could judge and impose penalties for disciplinary offences and misdemeanours committed by professorss and students, while the Council of Deans and the Rector were responsible for the final sentence. Strongly criticised by students, in particular for its punitive nature, which prevented individuals from working in the public sector or, if retired, from receiving a state pension[16], the court was abolished by decree shortly after the establishment of the Republic on 23 October 1910, and all cases previously dealt with by the academic police were transferred to the ordinary justice system[17]. However, persistent disciplinary problems led to its reinstatement in 1911, as previously mentioned.

This article assesses the conditions for the politicisation of the academic police case by the media, which took place within the framework of the transition to a modern and secularised republican education system, in parallel with increasing student protests

---

Moderna. 42. p. 129-149; Maria Paz Alonso Romero (2002) - *El fuero universitário salmantino (siglos XIII-XIX)*. p. 63-90; Ignacio Ruíz Rodríguez (1996) – "Fuero académico en las universidades americanas em la época de los Austrias", *Estudios de Historia Social y Económica de América*, nº 13. p. 77-86.

[14] António Vasconcelos (1987) - "Génese e evolução histórica do foro académico da Universidade portuguesa; extinção do mesmo 1290-1834". In *Escritos vários relativos à Universidade Dionisiana*. Reedição preparada por Manuel Augusto Rodrigues, vol. I, Coimbra: Arquivo da Universidade de Coimbra. p. 326-334.

[15] *Legislação Academica* |...|. *ob. cit.*. p. 222-233.

[16] Ana Maria Bandeira (2006) - "Têm a palavra os documentos: disciplina e polícia académica na Universidade de Coimbra". In *Archivum et Jus, Ciclo de Conferências 2004, Outubro – 2005, Abril, Actas*, Coimbra: Arquivo da Universidade de Coimbra. p. 139-140.

[17] "Uso de capa e batina, casos que até agora eram regulados pelo fôro académico da Universidade de Coimbra" (1910). In *Bibliotheca Democratica de Legislação. Periodico Jurídico*. nº 3, Anno I. p. 23.

based on various political and ideological perspectives, including anti-clericalism and republican radicalism.

To this end, the primary sources used were the documents available in the University of Coimbra Archives, most of which are handwritten, and include the academic police case files, age certificates (documents that applicants to the University had to present at enrolment to confirm that they met the age requirement for admission), Enrolments in Law (1911-1916), Exams (1911-1916), the Proceedings of the Congregations of the Faculty of Law (1912-1919) and the Professors' Files. This documentation was cross-referenced with other types of records, in particular academic and mainstream periodicals, university yearbooks and other sources.

From a theoretical point of view, the perspective chosen here focuses on contextualising the discourses in space and time, emphasising their dissemination and reception, and drawing on concepts and reflections proposed by Peter Burke[18] and Roger Chartier[19], among others, to interpret them.

Student protest and women's access to higher education: the state of the art

The subject of women in universities in Europe became a research topic from the 1980s onwards, coinciding with the emergence of women's and gender studies and their establishment as an academic discipline, the consolidation of democracies in Europe, and the increasing numbers of women entering higher education as students and professors, although occasional studies had been produced in

---

[18] Peter Burke (2008) - *What is cultural history?*, 2nd ed., Cambridge UK; Malden MA: Polity Presse.

[19] Roger Chartier (2002) - *A história cultural entre práticas e representações*, Lisbon: Difel.

earlier decades[20]. However, there has been a significant increase in the number of studies, especially since the 2000s, following Community legislation on European social policy and initiatives to promote social inclusion and combat discrimination, particularly as defined in the Treaty of Amsterdam in 1997 and the EU Charter of Fundamental Rights in 2000[21], reflecting the political importance attached to the issue of women in science and technology and its promotion among young people, especially girls. This research aims to highlight the contribution of women to the formalisation and institutionalisation of disciplinary fields in a range of academic areas and to recover the female "pioneers" and the chronologies of their admission to higher education, as well as the different entry methods or arguments for including or excluding women from academia in different fields of knowledge, thus developing an understanding of their different forms of scientific production[22].

The available studies show that women began to enter higher education in the second half of the 19th century[23]. It was a slow, prolonged process, both transnational and solitary, taking place "one by one", in the words of Flecha Garcia[24], but extending to most European countries, the United States of America and various

[20] Pilar Ballarín Domingo (2010) -"Entre ocupar y habitar. Una revisión historiográfica sobre Mujeres y Universidad en España". In *Arenal*, julio-diciembre, 2010.

[21] J. Cuesta Bustillo; Cristina García Nicolas (2007) - "Mujeres y ciencia en el espacio europeo de educación superior" In *Nuevos enfoques para la enseñanza de la historia*, Madrid. p. 215-218.

[22] Irene Vaquinhas (2019) - "História das mulheres e de género em Portugal: horizontes temáticos e desafios atuais". In *Género na arte. Corpo, sexualidade, identidade, resistência, Faces de Eva. Estudos sobre a Mulher*, Lisboa, nº extra. p. 44; Consuelo Flecha García (2010) - "Profesoras en la Universidad. El tránsito de las pioneras en España". In Arenal: Revista de historia de las mujeres. Vol. 17, Nº 2. p. 255-297.

[23] R. Pfefferkorn (2017) - "L'entrée des femmes dans les universités européennes : France, Suisse et Allemagne". In *Raison présente*. p. 117; Amélie Puche (2020) - "L´accès des femmes aux universités (1850-1940)". In *Encyclopédie d´histoire numérique de l´Europe* |en ligne.

[24] Consuelo Flecha García (2019) - "Barreras ante las pioneiras universitárias: uma mirada transnacional". In *CIAN-Revista De Historia De Las Universidades*, *22*(1). p. 21.

countries in South America such as Peru[25] at different times, sometimes earlier and sometimes later[26]. This international development has already been mapped out in comparative terms[27].

The studies also show that, although there were no legal bans on women entering universities, and the law was usually silent on the matter, these pioneers have obliged to submit formal applications, a procedure that applied in Russia as well as in Finland or Denmark, among other countries. The situation was no different in Portugal, where the conditions, chronologies and ways of integrating women into higher education were already established[28]. The regular and continuous admission of the first woman to the University of Coimbra, at that time the only university in Portuguese territory, dates back to the academic year 1891-1892, although the admission of women to higher education had actually begun in the School of Medicine and Surgery

---

[25] O. Valladares Chamorro (2012) - "La incursión de las mujeres a los estudios universitários". In *CIAN-Revista De Historia De Las Universidades*. 15 (1). p. 105-106.

[26] J. Cuesta Bustillo (2019) - "Presentación. Las mujeres querían ser doctoras, abogadas, y mucho más". In *CIAN-Revista De Historia De Las Universidades*, 22 (1). p. 11-12.

[27] Natalia Tikhonov Sigrist (2009) - "Les femmes et l'université en France, 1860-1914" In *Histoire de l'éducation* [En ligne], 122 |; Ana Guil Bozal; Consuelo Flecha García (2015) - "Universitarias em España: "De los inícios a la actualidad". In *Revista de Historia de la Educación Latinoamericana*, vol. 17, N° 24, enero-junio. p. 125-148; Consuelo Flecha García (2019) - "Barreras ante las pioneras universitarias: una mirada transnacional". In *CIAN-Revista De Historia De Las Universidades*, 22 (1). 19-59; P. Domínguez Prats & J. Cuesta (2019) - "Women in Academia from the 19th to the 21st Century". In *Culture & History Digital Journal, 8*(1). 001; Amélie Puche (2020) - "L'accès des femmes aux universités (1850-1940)". In *Encyclopédie d'histoire numérique de l'Europe* [en ligne]; R. Pfefferkorn (2017) - "L'entrée des femmes dans les universités européennes : France, Suisse et Allemagne". In *Raison présente*. p. 201, 117-127; Alicia Itatí Palermo (2006) - "El acceso de las mujeres a los estudios universitarios (siglo XIX)". In *Tebeto: Anuario del Archivo Histórico Insular de Fuerteventura*. n° 19. p. 375-417.

[28] Cândido dos Santos (s. d.) - *A mulher e a Universidade do Porto*, Porto: Universidade do Porto, A propósito do Centenário da Formatura das Primeiras Médicas Portuguesas. p. 11-12; Joaquim Ferreira Gomes (1987) - *A mulher na Universidade de Coimbra*, Coimbra: Livraria Almedina; Ana Maria Leitão Bandeira; João Rui Rocha Pita (1990) - "As primeiras mulheres farmacêuticas na Universidade de Coimbra". In *Kalliope, De Medicina*, n° 3. p. 21-28; Irene Vaquinhas (2018) - "Mulheres na Universidade de Coimbra: o caso das primeiras estudantes cabo-verdianas" / "Women at the University of Coimbra: the case of the first Cape Verdean female students". In *História. Revista da FLUP*, Porto, IV Série, Vol. 8, n° 1. p. 221-227.

in Porto in the academic year 1884-1885[29]. In the case of the Faculty of Law, the first woman would enrol in the academic year 1910-1911, although the presence of women in the Faculty remained low (19) throughout the First Republic (1910-1926), representing approximately 6.4% of the total number of female students (297) who enrolled at the University of Coimbra during the period under consideration[30].

As women began to enter European universities, their presence became more numerically representative but still marginal compared to male students, ranging from 3% to 20% of the student population between 1900 and 1920[31].

In the case of Portugal, the percentages are lower than in other European countries, as can be seen from Prata's studies on the First Republic (from 1910 to 1926)[32]. Female students accounted for about 1% of the total student population, although they registered higher annual increases than their male colleagues[33], which can be explained by the call-up for the First World War and the outbreak of pneumonic influenza, among other factors. The creation of the universities of Lisbon and Porto in 1911, by decrees issued on 22 March and 19 April, led to an increase in the number of female students in higher education, particularly in the newly created universities[34], a situation that would have been facilitated by the professional recognition of women working in certain fields or the possibility of women applying for employment in the public sector.

---

[29] Irene Vaquinhas (2018), *art. cit.*. p. 222.

[30] Ana Marcella de Carvalho (2019) - *As mulheres na Universidade de Coimbra ao tempo da Primeira República (1910-1926)*, Coimbra: FLUC, Master's dissertation. p. 138-147.

[31] Natalia Tikhonov Sigrist, *art. cit.*. p. 53-54; Puche, *art. cit.*. 2020.

[32] Manuel Alberto Carvalho Prata (2002) - *Academia de Coimbra (1880-1926). Contributo para a sua história*, Coimbra: Imprensa da Universidade. p. 33.

[33] Ana Marcella de Carvalho, *ob. cit.*. p. 58.

[34] Maria Cândida Proença (2002) - "A República e a educação". In *A crise do sistema e a implantação da República. Actas do Seminário realizado na Biblioteca Municipal Bento de Jesus Caraça*, Moita, 3 October 2000, Câmara Municipal da Moita. p. 57-59.

The family, social, academic (students and professors), institutional and ideological obstacles and resistance to the admission of women to universities is a subject that has been widely discussed at international level in recent years. In this area, the studies by Flecha Garcia[35] and Casals[36], among others, stand out, highlighting the legal mechanisms that acted as barriers or the prejudices that prevailed, which are directly linked to the patriarchal social order that considered women to be men's helpers and whose main duty was to serve and look after the family[37].

In Portugal, although many authors were opposed to women pursuing scientific and political careers because of their potential "masculinisation" or "the transformation of their gentle feelings into bitter passions"[38], some of the more enlightened sectors of public opinion, especially those with links to republican circles, favoured their admission to higher education, seeing it as a corollary of the struggle to extend civil rights and the need to develop scientific and secular education that would meet the requirements of bourgeois society and nation states, and even professional recognition. Admissions increased during the First Republic, spurred on by the actions and theoretical reflections of feminist associations, which saw women's education as a priority for the dignity and emancipation of women[39].

---

[35] Consuelo Flecha García (2019) - *art. cit..* ; Consuelo Flecha García (2021) - "Soñando el futuro. Mujeres estudiantes y profesionales en Cádiz en torno a 1900". In *Revista De Estudios Socioeducativos. ReSed*, (9).

[36] Q. Casals (2007) - "El acceso de las mujeres a la Universidad en España: el caso de las primeras universitarias leridanas (1882-1920)". In *CIAN-Revista De Historia De Las Universidades*, 20 (2). p. 275-301.

[37] Sigrist, *art. cit..* p. 53-54.

[38] D. Antonio da Costa (1892) - *A Mulher em Portugal, Obra posthuma publicada em beneficio de uma creança*, Lisbon: Typographia da Companhia Nacional Editora. p. 412.

[39] Maria Cândida Proença, *art. cit..* p. 59; Maria João Mogarro; Joaquim Pintassilgo (2013) - "Educação da mulher". In *Dicionário de História da I República e do Republicanismo*, vol. I: A-E, Lisbon: Assembleia da República. p. 1083-1085.

The relationship between the growing numbers of women in universities and changes in the context, gender relations and student protest has not received much attention from historians, with the exception of the more progressive periods of the 20th century, particularly the 1960s and/or 1970s[40].

For the mid-19th century and early 20th centuries, studies have focused mainly on the forms of student and professor association and mobilisation and their contribution to "the political and cultural construction of political modernity and its conflicts"[41]. As various authors have pointed out, student protests were common at the beginning of the 20th century, especially when they were based on specific academic demands, as was the case in Spain[42]. Whether or not linked to ideological causes such as freedom of expression and secularism, this type of protest represented an embryonic form of politicisation, although it would disappear after 1917-1918[43]. By reinforcing the key role of young people, the First World War had increased their civic awareness, non-conformism

---

[40] Marc Baldó Lacomba (2012) - "La rebelión de los estudiantes". In *Matrícula y leciones. XI Congreso Internacional de Historia de las Universidades Hispânicas*, Valencia Noviembre 2011, vol. I, Universidad de Valencia. p. 233-249; R. Morder (2018). "Transformations des mondes et mouvements étudiants". In *Matériaux pour l'histoire de notre temps*. 127-128. p. 10-15; M. Moreno Seco (2020) - "Universitarias en el antifranquismo. Mujeres, movilización estudiantil y feminismo, 1960-1975". In *CIAN-Revista De Historia De Las Universidades*, 23 (1). p. 55-85; Antonin Dubois (2022) - "La historiografía de los estudiantes en Europa, 1800-1945. Algunas perspectivas comparativas". In *CIAN-Revista De Historia De Las Universidades*, 25 (1). p. 11-12.

[41] Marc Baldó Lacomba; Germán Perales Birlanga (2022) - "Consideración sobre los estudiantes universitários españoles de 1800 a 1950". In *CIAN-Revista De Historia De Las Universidades*, 25 (1). p. 202.

[42] The student movement in Coimbra goes back a long way. In the 19th century, there were periods of great unrest, such as those of 1828-1834 and 1846. However, it was in the 20th century that protest became more intense, accompanying the crisis at the end of the monarchy and the affirmation of republican ideas, Fernando Taveira da Fonseca (2017) – "Portuguese Universities: Historiographical Overview" In *CIAN-Revista De Historia De Las Universidades*, 20 (1). p. 269.

[43] Eduardo González Calleja (2005) - "Rebelión en las aulas: um siglo de movilizaciones estudiantiles en España (1865-1968)". In *Ayer* 59 (3). p. 24; 30.

and aspirations for political reform, which were expressed through violent means[44].

With regard to Portugal, studies by Torgal and others have shown that in the case of Coimbra, the transition from the 19th to the 20th century was marked by strong criticism of university traditionalism and corporatism, mainly conveyed through a republican ideology, by both students and "scientific" professors. The latter advocated a university based on the Humboldtian model, which would be more rational and scientific in teaching and research, less "dogmatic, and distant from Catholic and ecclesiastical rituals", and with greater autonomy in relation to the central authority[45].

Student activism took the form of riots and strikes – such as the student strike of 1907, with national repercussions[46] – or by founding or working for the academic press, which had a different, distinctly opinionated, if not insurrectionary, political and ideological orientation[47]. In general, academic conflicts were associated with demands for a new model of public education, as opposed to a pedagogical system that was branded anachronistic, conservative and "Jesuit". The Faculty of Law was the main target, criticised for its authoritarian educational policies and the "despotism" of its teaching staff[48].

As in other cases in Europe, such as the Catholic universities of Paris, Toulouse or Valencia, until the beginning of the 20th century,

---

[44] Miguel Ángel Ruiz Canicer (2005) - "Estudiantes, cultura y violencia política en las universidades españolas (1925-1975)". In J. Muñoz; J. L. Ledesma; J. Rodrigo (Coord.) *Culturas y políticas de la violência: España siglo XX*, Madrid: Siete Mares. p. 251.

[45] Luís Reis Torgal (2013) - "Universidade de Coimbra". In *Dicionário de História da I República e do Republicanismo*, vol. III: N-Z, Lisbon: Assembleia da República. p. 1054-1055.

[46] Maria Neves Leal Gonçalves (2007) - "A greve académica de 1907. Suas repercussões políticas e educacionais". In *Revista Lusófona de Educação*, 9. p. 61-84.

[47] Manuel Alberto Carvalho Prata, *ob. cit.*. p. 288-298; Fernando Taveira da Fonseca, *art. cit.*. p. 268-269.

[48] Luís Reis Torgal, *art. cit.*. p. 1053.

the most prestigious faculties were those that taught jurisprudence[49] and attracted the most students, although the creation of a Faculty of Law in Lisbon in 1911 would reduce this and put an end to Coimbra's monopoly on the study of legal science[50].

After the establishment of the Republic, the student mood became more intense in terms of political and ideological confrontation, reflecting the plurality of views that were essentially shared by Portuguese society at the time, ranging from republican radicalism to more moderate, reformist positions[51], and "Catholic-monarchist" and integralist conservatism[52]. As França Amado, one of the city's leading booksellers, explained in a survey of "What Coimbra reads", organised by a local periodical, Charles Maurras (1868-1952), the founder of the *Action Française* movement and a theorist of nationalisms, was one of the city's most respected authors[53]. This is in line with several reports in the press that the monarchist tendency was dominant in academia and that there was also a significant core group of integralists[54], in addition to the political paths adopted by the student protests, which included support for "fascism or the New State"[55].

---

[49] Irene Vaquinhas; Maria Manuela Tavares Ribeiro (2020) - "Os estudantes da Universidade de Coimbra da reforma pombalina à implantação da República, 1772-1910 / Students of the University of Coimbra from the Pombaline Reform to the Founding of the Republic, 1772-1910 / Les étudiants de l'Université de Coimbra de la réforme pombaline à la République, 1772-1910". In *Ler História*, n° 76. p. 55-79.

[50] Manuel Alberto Carvalho Prata, *ob. cit.*. p. 49.

[51] Ernesto Castro Leal (2011) - "O campo político dos partidos republicanos portugueses (1910-1926)". In ***República, Republicanismo e Republicanos Brasil. Portugal. Itália***. Armando Malheiro da Silva; Carneiro, Maria Luiza Tucci, Salmi, Stefano (Org.), Coimbra: Imprensa da Universidade de Coimbra. p. 245-272.

[52] *Jornal de Coimbra*, 13 and 22 Jun. 1916.

[53] *Jornal de Coimbra*, 1 Jun. 1916.

[54] *Jornal de Coimbra*, 22 Jun. 1916.

[55] Luís Reis Torgal (2010) - "A República e a instrução pública: o caso do ensino superior". In *Biblos*, FLUC, VIII. p. 138.

The intersection between gender issues, rebellion and violence was less evident, especially in the case of young women, who were usually associated with a stereotype of docility and submission[56], even though the Republican period had provided an opening for challenging power relations, thus empowering the female sex to act as a historical subject and incorporating violence into youth culture as a strategic resource in the political struggle.

The link between feminism and pacifism, which had been common in the period before the Great War, came to an end as many associations rallied in favour of intervention in the war and the promotion of patriotism and nationalism[57]. This was the case with Portuguese associations, including the Portuguese Women's Crusade (*Cruzada das Mulheres Portuguesas*), which considered "male and female sacrifice on an equal footing"[58].

An anatomy of "disrespect for professors": contexts, protagonists and their political and ideological profiles

This case of "disrespect for professors", as it was called in the local press, instigated by the student Aurora Teixeira de Castro[59], took place in a university that was in the midst of institutional restructuring and still adapting to the changes imposed by the new legal framework introduced by the Republican regime and the implementation of the principles of the University Constitution of 19 April 1911.

---

[56] M. Moreno Seco; Bárbara Ortuño Martínez (2015) - "Presentación". In *Ayer* 100/2015 (4). p. 14-15; Adriana Cases Sola - "Mujeres rebeldes. Género, juventud y violência política em la Segunda Republica". In *Ayer* 100 (4). 76-77.

[57] Natividade da Conceição André Monteiro (2022) - *A mobilização das mulheres portuguesas durante a Grande Guerra (1914-1918)*, Lisbon: FCSH da UNL, PhD thesis. p. 68-70.

[58] Natividade da Conceição André Monteiro, *ob. cit.*. p. 71.

[59] *Gazeta de Coimbra*, 15 Mar. 1916.

In the academic year 1915-1916, the University of Coimbra had 1,565 students, 52 of whom were women[60] most of them studying at the Faculty of Letters, with only five studying law.

Born in the city of Porto on 2 June 1891, Aurora was the daughter of a private clerk[61]. In October 1912, she enrolled in the first-year subjects of the newly reformed curriculum, as well as the practical courses for each subject[62]. At the same time, she enrolled in the Faculty of Letters[63]. At the Faculty of Letters, she was a good student and received a distinction in some subjects[64], which entitled her to a scholarship for the academic year 1915-1916[65]. Her career at the Faculty of Law was not so illustrious: she was an average student whose marks ranged from mediocre to good. In 1916, a few days before she failed the exam that led to the police investigation, she had passed the exams in Tax Law and Administrative Law with grades of mediocre and satisfactory[66].

With regard to the exam she failed (the state exam in Economic and Political Sciences: Additional Paper), her indignation should also be interpreted in the light of the weighting of the two state exams – in economic and political sciences and in legal sciences – within the law course: it was necessary to pass the state exams in order to obtain a Bachelor of Law degree and to be eligible to work in the public sector. The exams were subject to specific regulations and were administered by a committee appointed by the government

---

[60] Manuel Alberto Carvalho Prata, *ob. cit.*. p. 33-34; Ana Marcella de Carvalho, *ob. cit.*. p. 121.

[61] UCA, Certidões de Idade, Cx. 4, 1901-1925.

[62] UCA, Inscrições Direito 1912-1916. Reforma de 1911, fl. 3v-4; *Anuário da Universidade de Coimbra*. 1912-1913. p. 173; 177; 181; 185.

[63] *Anuário da Universidade de Coimbra*, 1912-1913. p. 159-163.

[64] *Anuário da Universidade de Coimbra*, 1912-1913. Suplemento, s. p.

[65] *Anuário da Universidade de Coimbra*, 1915-1916. p. 47.

[66] UCA, Livro de Exames, Direito – Ciências Económicas e Políticas, 1915-1916, nº 45, fl. 43v; nº 46, fl. 57.

and presided over by a judge of a Court of First Instance, Court of Appeal, Supreme Court of Justice or Supreme Administrative Court[67]. In 1915-1916, of all the students (all male) who took the exam (157), 118 (75.2%) passed, 4 dropped out (2.5%) and only 35 (22.3%) failed. The year before, on 16 November 1915, she had passed the state exam in Political Law with a grade of good, which the Academic Board would take into account when deciding on her punishment. The pass rate of her male colleagues in this exam was very high: 96.3%.

Her colleague and husband, Jaime Augusto Cardoso de Gouveia[68], had also enrolled in the two faculties of Law and Letters and had obtained high grades, good and very good in almost all subjects, and distinctions in some, which enabled him to receive scholarships and exemption from fees for both courses from 1913-1914 onwards[69]. The other student involved in the police investigation, Fernando de Araújo[70], was an average student whose marks were usually considered sufficient. Like his colleagues, he also began studying law in the academic year 1912-1913[71].

The three students were therefore on the same course(s) and in the same age group, all between 25 and 30 years old. They were politically active, or at least very concerned, and subscribed to republican ideas. They used the media, in particular the republican newspapers *A Lanterna*, *A Revolta* and *A Montanha*, the latter being the organ of the Porto branch of the Portuguese Republican Party, to present democratic proposals or to create identities and

---

[67] *Anuário da Universidade de Coimbra*, 1913-1914. p. 339-342.

[68] Jaime Augusto Cardoso de Gouveia was born in Caria (in the municipality of Sernancelhe) on 16 November 1886, UCA, Certidões de Idade, Cx. 6, 1901-1925.

[69] *Anuário da Universidade de Coimbra*, 1914-1915. p. 66-67; *Anuário da Universidade de Coimbra*, 1915-1916. p. 44-45.

[70] Fernando de Araújo was born in the parish of Borbela in Vila Real on 23 January 1889, UCA, Certidões de Idade, Cx. 5, 1901-1925.

[71] UCA, Inscrições Direito 1912-1916. Reforma de 1911, fl. 92v-93.

define "the enemy". Their articles, especially those of the two male students, were mainly opinion pieces that could be categorised as party political journalism, given their aggressive and/or mordant tone and preference for what Júlia Leitão de Barros has aptly described as "debate as combat"[72].

Jaime Gouveia would also express his republican leanings when, as a student of the Faculty of Letters, he supported a protest against the provisions of the institution's disciplinary regulations of 14 January 1913, which forbade "the admission to classes of individuals not duly enrolled as students", on the grounds that this "is contrary to the spirit of the freedom of courses" and was "an attack on the integrity of open courses, which everyone is firmly in favour of maintaining"[73]. Republican pedagogical proposals favoured experimental reform and popular lifelong education for adults, principles that were embedded in the basic programmes of the popular and/or free universities created during this period, whose basic arguments were outlined in this student protest.

Aurora de Castro Gouveia's militant side centred on feminism, which she described as "a just and entirely defensible cause" in an article she wrote on "Feminist Politics of the Republic"[74]. She was also a member of the Portuguese Women's Crusade (*Cruzada das Mulheres Portuguesas*), a movement to support soldiers called up for war and their families, founded in March by Elzira Dantas Machado, the wife of the then President of the Republic[75].

The exam jury who failed Aurora Teixeira de Castro, presided over by a judge, was composed of Dr. António Faria Carneiro Pacheco (1887-1957), full professor at the Faculty of Law, and the

---

[72] Júlia Leitão de Barros (2021) - *O jornalismo republicano radical: O Mundo, 1900-1907*, Lisbon: Instituto Politécnico de Lisboa. p. 224-225.

[73] UCA, Letras. Reclamações. 1913.

[74] *A Montanha*, 5 Oct. 1916.

[75] Natividade da Conceição André Monteiro, *ob. cit.*, 2º vol.. Anexo 11.

graduates Domingos Fezas Vital (1888-1953) and João Maria Telo de Magalhães Colaço (1893-1931), both assistant lecturers at the same Faculty. Hence, they were all professors at the start of their careers and close in age to the students in question: the first had begun his career as a professor on 21 November 1914, rising rapidly from assistant lecturer to full professor[76]. The other two had been appointed assistant lecturers[77]. On the day of the incident, Domingos Fezas Vital had already been appointed full professor, a position he would take up on 25 January 1918[78], while João Maria Telo de Magalhães Colaço had been appointed associate professor the same year[79].

All three professors were therefore in positions of power and were embarking on influential careers that would allow them to benefit from the symbolic capital conferred on those who taught at a prestigious university, as well as the possibility of gaining access to high-level public positions, which would prove to be the case under the *Estado Novo* regime. Among other positions he held, António Faria Carneiro Pacheco was appointed Minister for Public Instruction in 1936 and was the person most responsible for the education sector under Salazar[80]. In 1918, the three professors, along with Oliveira Salazar, were suspended from the University for political reasons[81].

Two members of the jury (António Faria Carneiro Pacheco and Domingos Fezas Vital) appear in reports of other clashes, or at least

---

[76] During the period 16 May 1913 to 19 January 1914. UCA, Processos de Professores, Cx. 195.

[77] On 6 March 1915. *Diário do Govêrno*, II série, nº 64, 19 Mar. 1915.

[78] On 15 July 1916, UCA, Processos de Professores, Cx. 388.

[79] In 11 March 1916, UCA, Processos de Professores, Cx. 40 A.

[80] Maria Cândida Proença (1996) - "Pacheco, António Faria Carneiro (1887-1957)". In *Dicionário de História do Estado Novo* (Dir. Fernando Rosas; J. M. Brandão de Brito, Lisbon: Círculo de Leitores, Vol. II. p. 709.

[81] *Memoria Professorum..., ob. cit.*, p. 150.

tensions, involving students, in 1916 and in previous years, which were also dealt with by the academic police. A general reading of the four case files confirms that the reason for the clashes was always the same – a student had failed an exam or had to repeat it – although the students' insubordination took different forms, ranging from insults and to the use of the press to publicise the case, to direct attacks[82]. The most serious incident, which took place in October 1920, was described as an attempted homicide with a firearm against Dr. António Faria Carneiro Pacheco, although he was not shot, and the case was referred to the ordinary courts[83]. Either for this reason or for some other unspecified motive, on 23 August 1921 the professor was transferred "at his request" to the Lisbon Faculty of Law.

The use of weapons by students or, in this case, a professor, was relatively common at the time and can be associated with the practice of duels in journalistic and political circles, particularly among parliamentarians[84]. It occurred in a context of intense civil and political polarisation involving republicans and/or monarchists, and a climate of great instability, fear and discontent. As J. B. Serra observes, the period 1915-1919 "saw a very high number of military coups in political life"[85], which increased insecurity and the need for personal protection.

In the academic police proceedings, the possession, use and carrying of weapons was never questioned, including the assumption that the assistant lecturer Domingos Fezas Vital had acted as

[82] UCA, Processos de Polícia Académica.

[83] Júlio Ramos (1995) - "Um processo da Polícia Académica no Século XX. O atentado contra o Doutor Carneiro Pacheco". In *Alta de Coimbra. Que futuro para o passado? Actas do 2° Encontro sobre a Alta de Coimbra, realizado em 22 e 23 de Outubro de 1994*, Coimbra: GAAC-Grupo de Arqueologia e Arte do Centro. p. 196-209.

[84] Mário Matos e Lemos (1993) - "O duelo em Portugal depois da implantação da República". In *Revista de História das Ideias*, vol. 15. p. 561-597.

[85] João B. Serra, *art. cit.*. p. 117.

a member of the jury for Aurora de Castro Gouveia 's exam with "a pistol in his pocket", a situation that would be mentioned in disapproving tones in articles in the republican press. Regarding the type of firearm used by the professor, the documents simply state that it was a "pistol". A search carried out at the Civil Government Documentation Centre in Coimbra for "Applications and records of licences issued for the use and bearing of arms 1894-1926" failed to find any licence issued in his name[86].

In a university where "the monarchists are in command" and there were only "a handful" of republicans"[87], the two professors were regarded as Catholics, monarchists, "reactionaries" and "openly anti-republican". In fact, Domingos Fezas Vital, a member of *Acção Católica*, had accompanied Paiva Couceiro (1861-1944) in the monarchist attacks on the republican regime and had gone into exile in France and Spain, where he remained until 1914. On his return to Portugal, Vital joined the Faculty of Law at the University of Coimbra in 1915 as an assistant lecturer, as previously mentioned, while writing his PhD thesis[88].

In the case of António Faria Carneiro Pacheco, from early on, as Maria Cândida Proença has pointed out, "his right-wing, authoritarian tendencies became evident, after leading a student movement in 1908 that defended the use of dictatorial policies to solve the country's problems"[89].

The criticism levelled against these professors, who were considered typical representatives of the conservative model of social order,

---

[86] Cesário José Santos Quinteiro (2022) - *Coimbra e as Armas no início do século XX (1890-1925): Análise de documentação do Governo Civil de Coimbra*, FLUC, academic study.

[87] *A Montanha*, 10 Aug. 1916.

[88] "Os nossos mortos. Dr. Fezas Vital" (1953). In *Gazeta dos Caminhos de Ferro*, nº 1563, Ano LXV, 1 Feb. 1953. p. 471; Manuel Braga da Cruz (1996) - "Vital, Domingos Fezas (1888-1953)". In *Dicionário de História do Estado Novo*, Dir. Fernando Rosas; J. M. Brandão de Brito, Lisbon: Círculo de Leitores, vol. II. p. 1018.

[89] Maria Cândida Proença (1996), *art. cit.*. p. 709.

was not intended to be academic but was primarily of a political and ideological nature. This reinforced the personal dimension of the dispute, fuelled by the fact that they were in their twenties, a similar age to the students. Moreover, the periodicals were clear about this interpretation of the dispute: "the question under discussion here is not |...| strictly academic. It is a political question; it is blatant persecution of republicans who refuse to be bought"[90].

At the other extreme, among the most respected representatives of the University, there were references to "two fearless men from the Faculty of Law", namely Professors José Alberto dos Reis (1875-1955) and José Ferreira Marnoco e Souza (1869-1916)[91], especially the latter, who had died a few months earlier, in March 1916[92] and who was held in high esteem as a prime example of a university professor for his professional and scientific skills and for his pedagogical and human qualities. His opinions on the modernisation of higher education and the reform of legal studies[93], in addition to his contributions to the public debate on topics such as the "legitimacy or illegitimacy of resorting to government by dictatorship in the Portuguese legal-constitutional order, in the final phase of the monarchy (1907-1908)[94], or other controversial issues such as women's suffrage, made this law professor a kind of spiritual guide for the republican "academics". He declared himself in favour of votes for women arguing that "women's entry into economic life

---

90 *A Montanha*, 12 Aug. 1916.

91 *A Montanha*, 6 Aug. 1916.

92 *Gazeta de Coimbra*, 21 Mar. 1916.

93 Maria de Fátima da Cunha Moura Ferreira (2005) - *A institucionalização do saber jurídico na monarquia constitucional. A Faculdade de Direito da Universidade de Coimbra (1834-1910)*, 1° vol, Braga: Universidade do Minho – Instituto de Ciências Sociais. p. 76; 196.

94 Fátima Moura Ferreira (2012) - "Catedráticos de direito e política: o ideário reformador de Marnoco e Sousa sobre a crise do sistema político liberal" In separata de *Matrícula y Lecciones, XI Congreso Internacional de Historia de las Universidades Hispánicas*, Valencia, nov. 2011, vol. II, Universitat de València. p. 88.

necessarily requires their entry into political life", and that there was no "serious argument that could be presented against this reform", while at the same time confirming the legal ruling that allowed Carolina Beatriz Ângelo to vote in the 1911 elections[95].

"I am a lady!": gender stereotypes and representations

According to the 25 November 1839 Regulations, "lecturers, professors, heads of the various literary establishments, the Council of Deans and the auditor of the Faculty of Law"[96] were responsible for the functioning of the academic police. In the event that the offences in question could lead to more serious punishments, the defendants were "summoned to answer the charges made against them within forty-eight hours, with the option of presenting their defence, supported by any relevant documents or by the statements of two witnesses given orally in the presence of the Rector"[97]. Although, as mentioned above, the academic court was abolished under the First Republic, the accusatory procedure established in the 19th century regulations remained and students were responsible for preparing their own defence, in the form of a written plea submitted to the Academic Board.

This is what Aurora de Castro Gouveia did. In her statement, which was also to be published in the press[98], the argument was built around the accusation that she had "addressed Dr. Fezas Vital with insulting language, including the use of the word "coward"[99].

---

[95] José Ferreira Marnoco e Souza (1913) - *Constituição política da Republica Portuguêsa. Commentario*, Coimbra: F. França Amado Editor. p. 274-282.

[96] *Legislação Academica* |...|. *ob. cit.*. p. 224-225.

[97] *Legislação Academica* |...|. *ob. cit.*. p. 229.

[98] *A Montanha*, 1 Aug. 1916.

[99] UCA, Processo de polícia académica, 1916.

In her defence strategy, she neither claimed nor solicited what she described as the "attention due to her sex", or, in other words, she did not invoke femininity and modesty, the stereotypes of the normative gender discourse. On the contrary, she took responsibility for her actions, as an active subject, and demanded respect and consideration, proudly writing: "I am a lady! who has long been treated with an unjustifiable lack of respect by certain professors at the Faculty of Law, who seem to have forgotten the most rudimentary principles of courtesy due to a gentlewoman"[100]. She was probably referring to the fact that she had been ignored by Fezas Vital in the classroom, where she was the only woman present in groups of around three hundred students, a point which she also mentions.

Her relatively short and dry text responded to the accusation. She felt that she had been "|...| unfairly failed and that there was a clear intention on the part of the examiners to penalise me", essentially pointing the finger at Domingos Fezas Vital[101]. In her defence, she argued that her education had been based on study and hard work, citing the following: the fact that she had attended classes regularly, had made frequent use of the library and had consulted countless books on law; the grade she had obtained in the state exam she had passed, which had been the subject of informal praise from the Rector of the university "in a barber's shop in the city", and conveyed to her through her husband; the awards she had received at the Faculty of Letters, which had entitled her to a scholarship; the courses and diplomas she had obtained (as a primary school teacher and from the Institute of Commerce and Industry); testimonials of the merits of her work from the "most principled" professors of the practical classes - José Caeiro da Mata

[100] UCA, Processo de polícia académica, 1916. Aurora de Castro Gouveia's defense, fl. Iv.

[101] UCA, Processo de polícia académica, 1916. Aurora de Castro Gouveia's defense, fl. Iv.

(1877-1963), José Gabriel Pinto Coelho (1886-1978), Alberto da Cunha Rocha Saraiva (1886-1946) and the late Marnoco e Sousa[102]. She concluded by saying that she had never been failed or "outrageously favoured" by examiners[103].

Aurora then turned her attention to the exam she had failed, expressing her indignation at the change in the "legal" sequential order of the subjects being assessed, which differed from all previous exams, and at the fact that she had been questioned by the mentioned professor on material that was not included in the syllabus, an event also referred to in her husband´s document[104]. She also reproduced the questions she had been asked and the answers she had given. There is no mention in the testimonies of a similar situation involving male colleagues.

In this context, she stated that her assessment had been subject to discriminatory practices and difficulties created by the teaching staff, which she described as "malicious", "ostensibly in bad faith" and "unduly disrespectful".

She associated the negative assessment she had received to the "hostile" manner in which she had been treated by certain professors and to a "malicious" campaign to discredit her, in which at least one member of the jury had been involved. She based this statement on the fact that "at a conference to which I was invited", the speaker before her, the comedian Júlio Vilar, had, "(in his own words) at the request of Dr. Magalhães Colaço", recited "some mocking verses alluding to a certain D. Aurora"[105]. As further evidence of "Dr. Fezas'

[102] UCA, Processo de polícia académica, 1916. Aurora de Castro Gouveia's defense, fl. IV-IVv.

[103] UCA, Processo de polícia académica, 1916. Aurora de Castro Gouveia's defense, fl. IVv.

[104] UCA, Processo de polícia académica, 1916, Jaime Augusto Cardoso Gouveia's defense, fl. IV.

[105] UCA, Processo de polícia académica, 1916, Aurora de Castro Gouveia's defense, fl. VIIIv.

offensive behaviour", she added that he was "surrounded by a gang of political coreligionists who delight in provoking me and my husband", wondering whether "they obey the *mot d´ordre* of their leader?". She also added that when the said professor "passed me in the street |...|, if he was with anyone immune to ultramontane prejudice he would court me, but if he was accompanied by any of his "coterie" he would be certain not to greet me and would even be so rude as to turn his back on me", concluding that the professor "never knew how to behave consistently". This was why, when she saw "Dr. Fezas running away |...|", she called him a "coward"[106].

Although no explicit conflict can be inferred from this account, the student highlighted examples of gender bias and chauvinistic values which could take various forms, including some that were subtle but nonetheless vicious or oppressive.

In fact, Aurora de Castro Gouveia's presence at the university had not gone unnoticed, and the press had reported other examples of discriminatory behaviour and language, described as "persecution and humiliation", that the student had been subjected to. These included insults about her marriage to fellow student Jaime Augusto Cardoso de Gouveia, a former priest. According to the press, on the day of the wedding a large poster was put up at the main entrance to the university "inviting the public to jeer at the newlyweds and forbid them to enter the university". The year before, verses "written in red ink and containing crude insults" had appeared on various walls in the city of Coimbra, attacking the student's honour and dignity[107].

This behaviour was a reflection of the misogynistic environment that did not accept the student, even though she resisted the ideological barriers and gender-based exclusion created by professors or

---

106 UCA, Processo de polícia académica, 1916, Aurora de Castro Gouveia's defense, fl. IX.

107 *A Montanha*, 1 Aug. 1916.

her fellow students. Her defence, as a woman, also meant confronting the tyranny of social opinion, which aimed to discredit her personally and privately. At a time when feminism was a controversial issue for large sectors of society, identifying as a feminist constituted a deviant attitude that challenged the established codes and was in itself sufficient to provoke disagreement and disapproval.

The memorialist press of the time occasionally alluded to discriminatory behaviour on the part of professors regarding the presence of women in classes, either as part of the student body or in the adjacent galleries. It reported the case of a Philosophy of Law class attended by the feminist writer Guiomar Torresão (1844-1898) and the Condessa de Pomares, in which the professor responsible steered his lecture towards "the subject of bluestocking women, subjecting them to a thorough and scathing critique", causing the two women to leave. This prompted the professor to comment "They didn't like it. That's good", before returning to the original subject of his lecture[108].

The defence presented by Jaime Augusto Cardoso de Gouveia, her colleague and husband, accused of "insulting and publicly defaming the jury", was a of a legal nature. This student questioned the constituent elements of the crimes he was accused of committing in order to deny them, while stating that he was "only referring to facts that were already in the domain of public opinion". Specifically, during the exams the day before, the Professor Domingos Fezas Vital, whom he never named, had appeared in the exam room "with his betrothed" and, "to the astonishment of everyone", had "spent the entire examination period casting glances at her and signalling to the balcony" where "the woman was seated". He thus proceeded to discredit the Professor Domingos Fezas Vital, a defence strategy

---

[108] Alfredo de Leal (1931) - *Coimbra nos noventas e outras impressões*, Lisbon: Livraria Editora Guimarães & C.ª. p. 71-72.

which the couple both used, probably with the aim of reaching a consensus among the members of the university tribunal that would judge them. The other colleague, Fernando de Araújo, did not present a defence and no reasons were given in the case file.

The Academic Board unanimously condemned the three students. This university body, convened by the Vice-Rector of the University to examine the case and make a final decision, was made up of the dean professors of all faculties. Its meetings were held behind closed doors and there are no records. Only the final verdict was made public[109]. They were accused of "failing to pay due respect to the jury". They sentenced the two male students to expulsion from the University of Coimbra for two years in the case of Fernando de Araújo, and for one year in the case of Jaime Augusto Cardoso Gouveia, as the latter was "a distinguished student". As for Aurora Teixeira de Castro, the punishment was a "reprimand delivered by the Rector before the Faculty Council", with "the matter of her sex" and "her regular attendance at classes and the good grade she had been awarded in the previous state exam"[110] as mitigating factors.

The judicial handling of the case was therefore asymmetrical, reflecting F. Chauvaud's observation that "the functioning of justice |...| is also a "gender territory"[111]. It showed a leniency towards the female sex that seemed to reflect the collective representations and scientific and moral discourses of the time associated with women, which considered that their "nature" made them "weak", "morally timid" and "dependent" and therefore inferior and deserving of paternalistic clemency and, consequently, less penal and civil liability.

---

109 *Legislação Academica coligida pelo Dr. José Maria de Abreu e Coordenada, revista e ampliada pelo Dr. Antonio dos Santos Viegas* (1984), vol. I, 1772-1850, Coimbra, Titulo IV, 16°-20°. p. 229-230.

110 UCA, Processo de polícia académica, 1916, fl. 55-58.

111 Frédéric Chauvaud (2002) - "Introduction". In *Femmes et justice pénale : XIXe-XXe siècles* [en ligne], Rennes: Presses Universitaires de Rennes.

On an institutional level, the case had no consequences in the Faculty of Law and was not considered worthy of further attention. At a meeting of the Faculty of Law Council held on 8 August 1916, one of the members, without stating names, paid tribute to "the correct way in which everyone had administered the examinations", which was approved by the president of the meeting. The Director of the Faculty, in "expressing his thanks for the commendations", took the opportunity to state that he was "glad to hear of this, at a time when attempts had been made to create a disturbance over a simple decision by an exam jury"[112].

None of the students actually complied with the sentences or were even directly informed of them, as they had left Coimbra in August 1916 and the summonses issued by university's chief constable were delivered to their neighbours in their absence. The information was published by the press, with the added news that "the illustrious student Sra. D. Aurora |...| will not submit to the punishment stupidly imposed on her by these clownish professors"[113].

The following academic year, 1916-1917, the three students enrolled in the Faculty of Law of the University of Lisbon and graduated[114]. In the same year, Aurora de Castro Gouveia took the state exam that she had failed in Coimbra and passed with a score of ten[115]. After graduating in 1917, she and her husband opened a lawyer's office in Lisbon and began to work[116]. In 1921, at the

---

112 UCA, Actas das Congregações da Faculdade de Direito, 1912 a 1919, vol. 10, fl. 112v-113.

113 *A Montanha*, 10 Aug. 1916.

114 *Anuário da Universidade de Lisboa*, 1916-1917. p. 142; 144-145. When a student was expelled from the University of Coimbra, he had to leave. Continuing studies required enrollment at another university.

115 *A Montanha*, 3 Dec. 1916.

116 João Esteves (2005) - "Aurora Teixeira de Castro". In *Dicionário no Feminino (Séculos XIX-XX)*, Dir. Zília Osório de Castro and João Esteves, Coord. António Ferreira de Sousa *et alii*, Lisbon: Livros Horizonte. p. 158.

age of thirty, she was appointed deputy notary for the parish of Alcântara, in the district of Lisbon[117]. Although this was a profession to which women were admitted "late, and only reluctantly"[118] in several European countries. In Portugal, to judge by this case, they were admitted earlier, between twenty and thirty years sooner than in Scotland (1939), Spain (1942), France (1948), Belgium (1950) and other countries[119]. On the basis of this evidence, she would have been the first female public notary in Europe, or at least one of the first. In the 1920s she also became very active in feminism, joining various associations, including the Association for Feminist Propaganda (*Associação de Propaganda Feminista*) and the National Council of Portuguese Women (*Conselho Nacional das Mulheres Portuguesa*), participating in tributes to republican women and feminists (such as Adelaide Cabete, in 1926), and organising and attending conferences (such as the Congress on Feminism and Education in 1924, at which she delivered the opening speech), as well as writing books.

Jaime Gouveia, whom Aurora divorced in around 1926, worked as a lawyer before joining the Faculty of Law at the University of Lisbon in 1932, where he was appointed full professor in 1939[120]. In 1941 he faced disciplinary proceedings due to his interpretation of the question of divorce in the context of the Concordat signed

---

[117] *Diário do Govêrno*, II série. nº 184. 11 Aug. 1921.

[118] *Mapping the representation of women and men in legal professions across the EU* (2017), Bruxelles: Policy Department Citizen´s Rights and Constitutional Affairs. p. 24.

[119] Corinne Delmas - "Les notaires, le genre d'une profession à patrimoine". In *Travail, genre et sociétés*, 41, 2019. p. 128; Mercedes Pérez Hereza (2021) - "La mujer en el Notariado, reseña histórica, situación actual y perspectiva de futuro". In *El notário del siglo XXI* (96); Jean-Pierre Nandrin (2016) - "L'accès des femmes aux professions juridiques". In *Hommes et normes : Enjeux et débats du métier d'un historien*, Presses de l'Université Saint-Louis.

[120] António Ventura (2016) - *Silêncio e virtude. Uma história da Maçonaria Feminina em Portugal (1814-1990)*, Lisboa: Temas e Debates / Círculo de Leitores. p. 316-317.

by the Holy See and, after being suspended from his duties, became unemployed and without salary[121]. It was not possible to find any further information on Fernando de Araújo.

Reactions: the instrumentalisation of the academic police proceedings by the radical republican press

At a time of great political tension, when opinion papers such as *A Montanha* focused on controversial issues, "the monstruous crime committed by the University of Coimbra, which has ruined the careers of three distinguished students who are also ardent and committed republicans" became front-page news[122].

The newspaper adopted a belligerent, partisan stance, far from moderate, but typical of the radical republican press, as Júlia Leitão de Barros has clearly shown[123], reflected in headlines such as "The baseness of Coimbra", "Infamy without a name" and "The deeds of clowns"[124]. Within this "military frame of reference"[125], the paper would mount a "campaign" against the University of Coimbra in general and the Faculty of Law in particular, deploying rhetorical language to incite intransigence and violence in an attempt to discredit the institution, accusing it of being a "breeding ground for enemies of the regime", "medieval lair", "stamping ground for hypocrites and fanatics", "school for reactionaries" and "hotbed of anti-republican insurgency", run by "a band of Jesuits and villains",

---

121 Fernando Rosas; Cristina Sizifredo (2013) - *Estado Novo e Universidade. A perseguição aos professores*, Lisbon: Tinta da China. p. 83-84.

122 *A Montanha* 12 Sept. 1916.

123 Júlia Leitão de Barros, *ob. cit.*.

124 *A Montanha*, 12, 14, 20 Sept. 1916; 1, 15 Aug. 1916.

125 Júlia Leitão de Barros, *ob. cit.*. p. 225.

among other contemptuous descriptions[126]. Other cases involving students and the academic police were also recalled and dissected with little regard for objectivity or impartiality[127].

This action against the University of Coimbra, carried out by republican newspapers, aimed at a pragmatic response and a revival of the student "insurrectionary cycle" of the early 20th century, which included the student strike of 1907 and its serious political consequences, now urging the student population to mobilise around the proceedings against the three students. However, the lack of response from the student body would lead to alternative courses of action. The *A Montanha* columnists began asking questions: "And academia? Where is the soul of academia, so often in revolt against the arrogance and tyranny of the masters", in the words of Ernesto Almeida[128], echoed by his colleague Rui Moreno, who demanded: "Where is Academia and why does it not avenge these disgraceful attacks, remaining indifferent and silent when challenged by these vindictive and reactionary professors?"[129].

Having failed to launch a student uprising, the press opted for an offensive based on party loyalty and networks of influence. The newspaper *A Montanha* invited other radical republican periodicals, which it described as "liberal", to join the debate and, by reproducing articles or excerpts of articles and placing them at the centre of the "battle", broadened the political arena and launched a fierce attack on the university. It stirred up public opinion with texts from *A Resistência* (the organ of the Coimbra Democratic Republican Party), *A Voz da Justiça* (a Figueira da Foz republican weekly), the

---

126 *A Montanha*, 1, 12, 13 and 17 Aug. 1916.

127 *A Montanha*, 2 Aug. 1916.

128 *A Montanha*, 15 Aug. 1916.

129 *A Montanha*, 18 Aug. 1916.

Lanterna and *O Mundo*[130], many of which were written in response to headlines in the news and information-based press, including *A Opinião*, *A Capital* and the *Gazeta de Coimbra,* whose interpretation of events was more neutral and less politically committed, i.e. "conservative", according to *A Montanha*.

With the aim of showing support and solidarity to the three students who have been subjected to academic police proceedings, the republican newspapers also made use of local or regional republican party structures, as well as the "Republican galaxy" or, in other words, the relatively informal, grassroots republican and/or freemason organisations and groups[131], activating party affiliations, reciprocal relationships and networks based on clientelism and influence.

One of the first institutions to react to the republican newspapers' appeal was the women freemasons, through the Feminist Group for the Promotion and Defence of Women's Rights at the Carolina Ângelo Guild, a lodge founded in 1915 and headed by Ana de Castro Osório[132]. The well-known feminist immediately expressed her support for Aurora de Castro Gouveia in a letter she addressed to her, which was published by the press. In the letter she states "I write to assure you that there are Portuguese women on your side, in revolt against the tyranny and arrogance that assails you |...| and they will never abandon you"[133]. At the time, the student had not yet become a mason, although she would do so the following year, when she became a member of the aforementioned lodge[134].

---

130 *A Montanha*, 28 de Jul., 13, 17 Aug. 1916.

131 Maria Alice Samara (2009) - "O republicanismo" In *História da Primeira República Portuguesa*, Coord. Fernando Rosas; Maria Fernanda Rollo, Lisbon: Tinta da China. p. 68-71.

132 Fernando Marques da Costa (s. D.) - *A Maçonaria Feminina*, Lisboa: Editorial Vega, Lda.. p. 55.

133 *A Montanha*, 18 Aug. 1916.

134 When this Lodge closed, in 1922, she joined the Humanidade Lodge and, in 1926, the Humanidade do Direito Humano Lodge, where she adopted the symbolic

Also, in the context of masonic or masonic-related organisations, the Lisbon Civil Registry Association, through some of its members, issued a formal protest "against the failing" of the three students[135].

The organisational structures of the Republican Party were also involved in the "battle" against the Academic Board, for example via the motion approved by the Municipal Committee of the Republican Party of Vila Nova de Gaia condemning the "political behaviour of the assistant lecturers at the Faculty of Law, which does not earn them the right to be appointed full professors in the Faculty"[136]. The members of the "Dr. Afonso Costa" Devesas Democratic Centre in the same area, "in a general meeting" protested "against the punishments imposed"[137].

The decision of the Academic Board, known in the radical press as the "Inquisitorial Board", on the punishments imposed on the three students provided an opportunity for impassioned demands for the "purging" of the Faculty of Law of Coimbra and, in particular, for publicity for the campaign to establish a Faculty of Law in the city of Porto, a "recurring subject" in "representations to the Porto University Senate and in the northern social circles of the various republican governments"[138]. The press echoed these demands, or even calls for "investigations" and the closure or transfer of the faculty to the city of Porto, hoping to take advantage of the situation and the faded image that a certain sector of the press associated with the University of Coimbra[139]. The newspaper *A Montanha*, for

---

name of Madame Rolland. In 1924, as a mason, she established the triangle in the city of Portalegre, together with Adelaide Cabete and Arnaldo Brazão, Fernando Marques da Costa, *ob. cit.*. p. 57-58; 66-67; António Ventura, *ob. cit.*. p. 322-323.

[135] *Gazeta de Coimbra*, 2 Sep. 1916.

[136] *A Montanha*, 10 Sep. 1916.

[137] *A Montanha*, 20 Oct. 1916.

[138] Francisco Miguel Araújo; Luís Alberto Marques Alves (2013) - "Universidade do Porto" In *Dicionário de História da I República e do Republicanismo*, vol. III: N-Z, Lisbon: Assembleia da República. p. 1062.

[139] *A Montanha*, 1, 8, 15, 19 Aug., 1 Dec. 1916.

example, supported a localist project, that it had helped to set up and publicise. However, the controversy predates the well-known "Academic Question" which, in 1919, set the University of Coimbra against the University of Porto over the closure of the Faculty of Letters in Coimbra, on the grounds that it was "scholastic" (the dominant ecclesiastic education), and its transfer to the city of Porto, sparking protests.

From October 1916, the controversy between the academic board and the three students began to die down in the *A Montanha* newspaper. The more moderate and conservative newspapers began to pay more attention, especially in the city of Coimbra, to the requests, mainly from students, for the re-establishment of the university's academic traditions. These traditions had been suspended by republican legislation and extended to other higher education institutions in Portugal. They included the *praxes* (initiation rituals), academic dress (the *capa e batina,* or black cape and gown), the ringing of the Cabra bell and the PhD ceremonies, among others[140]. The newspaper *A Montanha* took advantage of the objections to the *praxes* linking the previous case to the present situation, to find new inspiration [141].

Final considerations

Aurora Teixeira de Castro is not an unknown woman. However, although her career as a feminist is well documented, little is known about her academic career and the beginnings of her involvement in politics, which coincided with the establishment of the First Republic. This was a period of intense polarisation and

[140] *Gazeta de Coimbra*, 23 Aug., 2 Sept., 29 Nov., 7, 20, 21 Dec. 1916.

[141] *A Montanha*, 30 Nov., 2 Dec. 1916.

division between monarchists and republicans, as well as within the republican forces themselves, which would deepen when Portugal entered the First World War. It was a period in which history seemed to be accelerating, ushering in a climate of debate and practical experimentation.

Admission to the University of Coimbra provided her with an unprecedented political apprenticeship and seems to have served as a means of gaining entry to republican organisations, particularly those with links to feminism, which she would use her talents to promote. Like her other male colleagues, she was skilful in gaining the backing of networks offering support and influence and knew how to take advantage of the power of the "fourth estate", the press.

According to the sources we researched, this episode did not lead to immediate changes at the Faculty of Law. However, in 1919, Carneiro Pacheco, as well as Fezas Vital, Magalhães Colaço (and Oliveira Salazar, who would later become President of the Council of Ministers during the Estado Novo) were suspended from their duties and subjected to an enquiry by the University of Coimbra. This was based on "hostility to the regime" on the part of the aforementioned professors in the exercise of their university teaching. Their guilt was not proven, but they were transferred to the University of Lisbon. On the other hand, "the failure of Aurora" was widely publicised by newspapers (national, regional, informative and of opinion, student, political). At the time, the press acted as an "amplifier of the female voice", as Isabel Lousada summarises. And in this case, it amplified its spatial and temporal reach[142].

---

[142] Vítor Neto (2016) - "Carneiro Pacheco, o estado corporativo e a União Nacional / Carneiro Pacheco, the corporative state and national union". In *História, pensamento e cultura. Estudos em homenagem a Carlos Cordeiro*, Coord. Manuel Sílvio Alves Conde; Susana Serpa Silva, Ponta Delgada. p. 135-152; Isabel Lousada (2010), "Imprensa: amplificador da voz feminina". In *Percursos, conquistas e derrotas das mulheres na 1ª República. Catálogo*, Lisboa: Câmara Municipal de Lisboa. p. 41-56.

The analysis of the documentation consulted for this research shows that it was not easy for women to gain access to law faculties and the legal profession. This was not only because this process was one of the slowest in Europe, but also because, in the case of Coimbra, it met with resistance from the university, at least from some professors and students.

In addition to the commonly accepted representations of women's nature and the social pressures exerted on them, there were also invisible expressions of intolerance and exclusion and a tense and violent local political context. The institutional response to this case, by devaluing it, also expresses the conformism of the hierarchical and androcentric university structure, which must be attributed to the acceptance of social mechanisms of impunity. Although equality was proclaimed in official republican discourse as a fundamental principle of social coexistence, there was resistance to its actual implementation. Aurora had to endure "everyday injustices" that required her to show resilience, self-confidence and the ability to fight, and move forward without allowing herself to be beaten by the difficulties she faced.

Identifying as a feminist, as she makes clear in the articles she wrote for the press, was a difficult process, especially at a time when the feminist was the subject of criticism and mockery and was defined in negative terms. The newspaper *O Radical,* for example, offered the following description: "the emaciated face with its unseemly wrinkles, the sloppy, unflattering dress, ill-fitting on her ungainly body, smiles ruined by glimpses of missing teeth: comrade x in a man's suit, wearing no perfume, no tenderness in her eyes – at best, an ugly man"[143].

As well as establishing herself as a feminist, Aurora also entered a profession that had previously been restricted to men. By

[143] *O Radical,* 9 May 1908.

questioning the curricular grading she had been given, she paved the way for a controversy at the University of Coimbra that would continue in the years immediately following her departure.

Sources and Bibliography

Manuscript sources

University of Coimbra Archive (UCA)

Actas das Congregações da Faculdade de Direito, 1912 a 1919, vol. 10.

Certidões de Idade, Caixa. 4 (1901-1925) – IV-1ª D-5-3-14; Caixa 5 (1901-1925) - IV-1ª D-5-3-15; Caixa 6 (1901-1925) - IV-1ª D-5-3-16;

Inscrições. Direito. 1912-1916. Reforma de 1911.

Letras. Reclamações. 1913.

Livro de Exames, Direito, Sciencias Economicas e Politicas. Prova complementar. Prova oral, nº55.

Livros de Exames, Direito, Ciencias Economicas e Politicas, nº 45 (de 2 Agosto 1915 a 11 Julho 1922); nº 46 (1914-1915).

Processos de Polícia Académica (1916-1920).

Processos de Professores: Vital, Domingos Fezas, Caixa 388; António Carneiro Pacheco, Caixa 195; João Maria Telo de Magalhães Collaço, Caixa 40A.

Governo Civil de Coimbra, Requerimentos e relações de concessão de licenças de uso e porte de armas 1894–1926.

Bibliography

"Os nossos mortos. Dr. Fezas Vital" (1953), *Gazeta dos Caminhos de Ferro*, nº 1563, 1 Feb., Ano LXV. p. 471.

"Sra. D. Regina Quintanilha" (1913), *Ilustração Portugueza*, II série, nº 405, 24 Nov..

A Montanha. Diario do Partido Republicano Português (1916-1921).

Adelaide Cabete, medica elvense. Homenagem de "A Fronteira" e dos seus admiradores, separata do jornal *A Fronteira*, 4 May 1924, Elvas: Tipografia Elvense.

Alonso Romero, Maria Paz (2002) - *El fuero universitário salmantino (siglos XIII-XIX)*, 2002, p. 63-90; https://eusal.es/index.php/eusal/catalog/download/978-84-7481-994-6/4992/3595-1?inline=1

Anuário da Universidade de Coimbra, 1911-1912 to 1915-1916; https://digitalis-dsp.uc.pt/republica/UCBG-8-118-1-3/rosto.html

Anuário da Universidade de Lisboa, Coordenado por António Joaquim Pereira Machado, Ano Lectivo de 1915-1916 (1917). 2ª Parte, Lisboa: Imprensa da Livraria Ferin; Ano Lectivo de 1916-1917 (1919). 2ª Parte, Lisboa: Imprensa Nacional e Ano Lectivo de 1917-1918 (1920). 1ª Parte, Lisboa: Imprensa Nacional.

Araújo, Francisco Miguel; Alves, Luís Alberto Marques (2013) - "Universidade do Porto", *Dicionário de História da I República e do Republicanismo*, vol. III: N-Z, Lisbon: Assembleia da República. p. 1060-1064.

Baldó Lacomba, Marc (2012) - "La rebelión de los estudiantes", *Matrícula y leciones. XI Congreso Internacional de Historia de las Universidades Hispânicas* (Valencia Noviembre 2011), vol. I. Universidad de Valencia. p. 233-249; https://www.academia.edu/5894648/LA_REBELION_DE_LOS_ESTUDIANTES

Baldó Lacomba, Marc; Perales Birlanga, Germán (2022) - "Consideración sobre los estudantes universitários españoles de 1800 a 1950", *CIAN-Revista De Historia De Las Universidades*, *25*(1). p. 193-228. https://doi.org/10.20318/cian.2022.6998

Ballarín Domingo, Pilar (2010) - "Entre ocupar y habitar. Una revisión historiográfica sobre Mujeres y Universidad en España", *Arenal*, julio-diciembre. p. 223-254: http://revistaseug.ugr.es/index.php/arenal/article/view/1450/1618.

Bandeira, Ana Maria (2006) - "Têm a palavra os documentos: disciplina e polícia académica na Universidade de Coimbra", *Archivum et Jus, Ciclo de Conferências 2004, Outubro – 2005, Abril, Actas*, Coimbra: Arquivo da Universidade de Coimbra. p. 123-150.

Bandeira, Ana Maria Leitão; Pita, João Rui Rocha (1990) - "As primeiras mulheres farmacêuticas na Universidade de Coimbra", *Kalliope, De Medicina*, nº 3. p. 21-28.

Barros, Júlia Leitão de (2021) - *O jornalismo republicano radical: O Mundo, 1900-1907*. Lisboa: Instituto Politécnico de Lisboa; http://hdl.handle.net/10400.21/13139

Bonino Méndez, Luis (1998) - "Micromachismos: La violencia invisible en la pareja"; http://www.joaquimmontaner.net/Saco/dipity_mens/micromachismos_0.pdf

Burke, Peter (2008) – *What is cultural history?*, 2nd ed., Cambridge UK; Malden MA: Polity Presse.

Carvalho, Ana Marcella de (2019) - *As mulheres na Universidade de Coimbra ao tempo da Primeira República (1910-1926)*. Coimbra: FLUC (Master's dissertation); http://hdl.handle.net/10316/86399

Casals, Q. (2017) - "El acceso de las mujeres a la Universidad en España: el caso de las primeras universitarias leridanas (1882-1920)". *CIAN-Revista De Historia De Las Universidades*, *20*(2). p. 275-301. https://doi.org/10.20318/cian.2017.3943

Cases Sola, Adriana (2015) - "Mujeres rebeldes. Género, juventud y violência política en la Segunda República", *Ayer* 100/2015 (4). p. 73-96; https://revistaayer.com/articulo/245

Castro, Aurora Teixeira de (1926) - *Monografia da cidade do Pôrto*. Lisboa: Composto e impresso na Secção de Publicidade do Museu Comercial.

Chartier, Roger (2002) - *A história cultural entre práticas e representações*, Lisboa: Difel.

Chauvaud, Frédéric (2002) - "Introduction" In "*Femmes et justice pénale : XIXe-XXe siècles"*[en ligne], Rennes: Presses universitaires de Rennes, 2002; https://doi.org/10.4000/books.pur.16197.

Costa, D. Antonio da (1892) - *A Mulher em Portugal, Obra posthuma publicada em beneficio de uma creança*, Lisboa: Typographia da Companhia Nacional Editora.

Costa, Fernando Marques da (s. d.) - *A Maçonaria Feminina*, Lisboa: Edtorial Vega, Lda.

Cruz, Manuel Braga da (1996) - "Vital, Domingos Fezas (1888-1953)", *Dicionário de História do Estado Novo*, Direcção de Fernando Rosas; J. M. Brandão de Brito, Vol. II. Lisboa: Círculo de Leitores. p. 1018.

Cuesta Bustillo, Josefina (2019) - "Presentación. Las mujeres querían ser doctoras, abogadas, y mucho más". *CIAN-Revista De Historia De Las Universidades*, *22*(1). p. 11-18. https://doi.org/10.20318/cian.2019.4798

Cuesta Bustillo, Josefina; García Nicolas, Cristina (2007) - "Mujeres y ciencia en el espacio europeo de educación superior", *Nuevos enfoques para la enseñanza de la historia*. Madrid. p. 211-230.

D. Regina Quintanilha (1913) - "O seu aparecimento como advogada nos tribunaes de Lisboa", *Occidente. Revista Illustrada de Portugal e do Estrangeiro*, XXXVI volume, 30 Nov 1913, nº 1257, 0368.

Decreto com força de lei de 19 de Abril de 1911, https://sigarra.up.pt/up/pt/legislacao_geral.ver_legislacao?p_nr=4095

Decreto de 22 de Março de 1911, *Diario do Gôverno*, nº 68, 24 de Março de 1911, fl. 1261-1262; https://files.dre.pt/gratuitos/1s/1911/03/06800.pdf

Delmas, Corinne (2019) - "Les notaires, le genre d'une profession à patrimoine", *Travail, genre et sociétés*, 41. p. 127-145. https://doi.org/10.3917/tgs.041.0127

Diário do Govêrno, I série, nº 16, 9 Agosto de 1921; II série, nº 64, 19 de Março de 1915.

Domínguez Prats, P., & Cuesta, J. (2019) - "Women in Academia from the 19th to the 21st Century". *Culture & History Digital Journal*, *8*(1), 001. Retrieved from https://cultureandhistory.revistas.csic.es/index.php/cultureandhistory/article/view/150

Dubois, Antonin (2022) - "La historiografía de los estudiantes en Europa, 1800-1945. Algunas perspectivas comparativas". In *CIAN-Revista De Historia De Las Universidades*, 25 (1). p. 5-21.

Esteves, João (2005) - "Aurora Teixeira de Castro", *Dicionário no Feminino (Séculos XIX-XX)*, Direção Zília Osório de Castro e João Esteves, Coord. António Ferreira de Sousa *et alii*. Lisboa: Livros Horizonte. p. 156-158.

Ferreira, Fátima Moura (2012) - "Catedráticos de direito e política: o ideário reformador de Marnoco e Sousa sobre a crise do sistema político liberal", separata de *Matrícula y Lecciones, XI Congreso Internacional de Historia de las Universidades Hispánicas (Valencia, noviembre 2011)*, vol. II. Universitat de València. p. 85-96; https://hdl.handle.net/1822/22922

Ferreira, Maria de Fátima da Cunha Moura (2005) - *A institucionalização do saber jurídico na monarquia constitucional. A Faculdade de Direito da Universidade de Coimbra (1834-1910)*, 1º vol., Braga: Universidade do Minho – Instituto de Ciências Sociais, https://repositorium.sdum.uminho.pt/bitstream/1822/23563/1/Tese%20Doutoramento%20Fátima%20Moura%20Ferreira.pdf

Flecha Garcia, Consuelo (2010) - "Profesoras en la Universidad. El tránsito de las pioneras en España", *Arenal: Revista de historia de las mujeres*, Vol. 17, Nº 2. p. 255-297; https://doi.org/10.30827/arenal.v17i2.1451

Flecha Garcia, Consuelo (2019) - "Barreras ante las pioneiras universitárias: uma mirada transnacional", *CIAN-Revista De Historia De Las Universidades*, *22*(1). p. 19-59. https://doi.org/10.20318/cian.2019.4799

Flecha, C. (2021) - "Soñando el futuro. Mujeres estudiantes y profesionales en Cádiz en torno a 1900". *Revista De Estudios Socioeducativos. ReSed*, (9); https://revistas.uca.es/index.php/ReSed/article/view/7413

Fonseca, Fernando Taveira da (2017) - "Portuguese Universities: Historiographical Overview" In *CIAN-Revista De Historia De Las Universidades*, *20*(1). p. 251-274. https://doi.org/10.20318/cian.2017.3734

Gazeta de Coimbra (29 July-31 Déc. 1916).

Gomes, Joaquim Ferreira (1987) - *A mulher na Universidade de Coimbra*. Coimbra: Livraria Almedina.

Gomes, Joaquim Ferreira (1991) - "Regina Quintanilha – a primeira caloira de Direito", *Estudos para a história da Universidade de Coimbra*. Coimbra. p. 57-73.

Gonçalves, Maria Neves Leal (2007) - "A greve académica de 1907. Suas repercussões políticas e educacionais", *Revista Lusófona de Educação*, 9. p. 61-84; https://revistas.ulusofona.pt/index.php/rleducacao/article/view/659

González Calleja, Eduardo (2005) - "Rebelión en las aulas: um siglo de movilizaciones estudiantiles em España (1865-1968), *Ayer* 59/2005 (3). p. 21-49; https://www.revistaayer.com/sites/default/files/articulos/59-1-ayer59_JuventudPoliticaEspanaContemporanea_GonzalezCalleja.pdf

Guil Bozal, Ana; Flecha García, Consuelo (2015) - "Universitarias em España: De los inícios a la actualidad", *Revista de Historia de la Educación Latinoamericana*, Vol. 17, Nº 24, enero-junio. p. 125-148.

Hernández Sánchez, Gustavo (2017) - "El fuero académico em la Real Universidad de México y otras atribuciones de su rectos: 1597-1640", *Cuadernos de Historia Moderna*, 42. p. 129-149.

Jornal de Coimbra. Bi-Semanario Republicano, 6º Ano, 1916.

Leal, Alfredo de (1931), *Coimbra nos noventas e outras impressões. Lisboa: Livraria Editora Guimarães & C.ª*.

Leal, Ernesto Castro (2011) - "O campo político dos partidos republicanos portugueses (1910-1926)", *República, Republicanismo e Republicanos Brasil. Portugal. Itália*, Silva, Armando Malheiro da; Carneiro, Maria Luiza Tucci, Salmi, Stefano (Org.). Coimbra: Imprensa da Universidade de Coimbra. p. 245-272; https://digitalis-dsp.uc.pt/bitstream/10316.2/31138/1/10-%20república,%20republicanismo.pdf

Legislação Academica coligida pelo Dr. José Maria de Abreu e Coordenada, revista e ampliada pelo Dr. Antonio dos Santos Viegas, vol. I, 1772-1850 (1894). Coimbra: Imprensa da Universidade; URI:http://hdl.handle.net/10316.2/3281

Lemos, Mário Matos e (1993) - "O duelo em Portugal depois da implantação da República", *Revista de História das Ideias*, vol. 15. p. 561-597; https://digitalis-dsp.uc.pt/bitstream/10316.2/42007/1/O_duelo_em_Portugal.pdf

Lousada, Isabel (2010) - "Imprensa: amplificador da voz feminina". *Percursos, conquistas e derrotas das mulheres na 1ª República. Catálogo*, Lisboa: Câmara Municipal de Lisboa. p. 41-56.

Mapping the representation of women and men in legal professions across the EU (2017), Policy Department Citizen´s Rights and Constitutional Affairs, Bruxelles; https://www.europarl.europa.eu/thinktank/en/document/IPOL_STU(2017)596804

Mattoso, José (1997) - "A universidade portuguesa e as universidades europeias", *História da Universidade em Portugal*. I vol. (1290-1536). Universidade de Coimbra / Fundação Calouste Gulbenkian. p. 3-29.

Memoria Professorum Universitatis Conimbrigensis. 1772-1937 (1992), vol. 2, Dir. Manuel Augusto Rodrigues. Coimbra: Arquivo da Universidade de Coimbra.

Mogarro, Maria João; Pintassilgo, Joaquim (2013) - "Educação da mulher", *Dicionário de História da I República e do Republicanismo*, vol. I: A-E. Lisboa: Assembleia da República. p. 1083-1087.

Monteiro, Natividade da Conceição André (2022) - *A mobilização das mulheres portuguesas durante a Grande Guerra (1914-1918)*. Lisboa: FCSH da UNL (PhD thesis).

Morder, Robi (2018) - "Transformations des mondes et mouvements étudiants". *Matériaux pour l'histoire de notre temps*, 127-128. p. 10-15. https://doi.org/10.3917/mate.127.0010

Moreno Seco, Monica; Ortuño Martínez, Bárbara (2015) - "Presentación", *Ayer* 100/2015 (4). p. 23-20; https://revistaayer.com/sites/default/files/articulos/100-0-ayer100_generojuventudcompromiso.pdf

Nandrin, Jean-Pierre (2016) - "L'accès des femmes aux professions juridiques". In *Hommes et normes: Enjeux et débats du métier d'un historien,* Presses de l'Université Saint-Louis. doi :10.4000/books.pusl.2897

Neto, Vítor (2016) - "Carneiro Pacheco, o Estado corporativo e a União Nacional / Carneiro Pacheco, the corporative state and national union". *História, pensamento e cultura. Estudos em homenagem a Carlos Cordeiro*, Coord. Manuel Sílvio Alves Conde; Susana Serpa Silva. Ponta Delgada. p. 135-152.

Our Legal Heritage: Scotland's first woman notary public joins prestigious list of pioneers; https://www.scottishlegal.com/articles/our-legal-heritage-scotland-s-first-woman-notary-public-joins-prestigious-list-of-pioneers

"Penas disciplinares para os alunos dos institutos de ensino dependentes da Direcção Geral da Instrucção Secundária, Superior e Especial", *Diário do Govêrno*. 24 Aug. 1911. In *Anuário da Universidade de Coimbra*. Ano lectivo de 1911-1912, Coimbra: Imprensa da Universidade, 1912. p. 148-149.

Pérez Hereza, Mercedes (2021) - "La mujer en el Notariado, reseña histórica, situación actual y perspectiva de futuro", *El notário del siglo XXI* (96); https://www.elnotario.es/opinion/opinion/10620-la-mujer-en-el-notariado-resena-historica-situacion-actual-y-perspectiva-de-futuro

Pfefferkorn, R. (2017) - "L'entrée des femmes dans les universités européennes : France, Suisse et Allemagne", *Raison présente*, 201. p. 117-127. https://doi.org/10.3917/rpre.201.0117

Prata, Manuel Alberto Carvalho - *Academia de Coimbra (1880-1926)* (2002) - *Contributo para a sua história*, 2 vols., Coimbra: Imprensa da Universidade.

Proença, Maria Cândida (1996) - "Pacheco, António Faria Carneiro (1887-1957)", *Dicionário de História do Estado Novo*, Direcção de Fernando Rosas; J. M. Brandão de Brito, Lisboa, Círculo de Leitores, Vol. II. p. 709-710.

Proença, Maria Cândida (2013) - "Ensino". In *Dicionário de História da I República e do Republicanismo*, vol. I: A-E. Lisbon: Assembleia da República, 2013. p. 1142-1148.

Proença, Maria Cândida (2002) - "A República e a educação", *A crise do sistema e a implantação da República, Actas do Seminário realizado na Biblioteca Municipal Bento de Jesus Caraça*, Moita, 3 Oct. 2000. Câmara Municipal da Moita. p. 37-63; https://www.cm-moita.pt/cmmoita/uploads/writer_file/document/1155/a_crise_do_sistema_liberal_e_a_implementa__o_da_rep_blica_pdf.pdf

Puche, Amélie (2020) - "L'accès des femmes aux universités (1850-1940)", *Encyclopédie d'histoire numérique de l'Europe* [en ligne], Permalien: https://ehne.fr/fr/node/14080

Quinteiro, Cesário José Santos (2022) - *Coimbra e as Armas no início do século XX (1890-1925): Análise de documentação do Governo Civil de Coimbra*, FLUC (academic work).

O Radical, 9 May 1908.

Ramos, Júlio (1995) - "Um processo da Polícia Académica no Século XX. O atentado contra o Doutor Carneiro Pacheco", *Alta de Coimbra. Que futuro para o passado? Actas do 2° Encontro sobre a Alta de Coimbra, realizado em 22 e 23 de Outubro de 1994*. Coimbra: GAAC-Grupo de Arqueologia e Arte do Centro. p. 185-210.

A Revolta, Ano 4°, n° 88, 29 Jul. 1916

Rosas, Fernando; Sizifredo, Cristina (2013) - *Estado Novo e Universidade. A perseguição aos professores*. Lisboa: Tinta da China.

Ruiz Carnicer, Miguel Ángel (2005) - "Estudiantes, cultura y violência política en las universidades españolas (1925-1975)", J. Muñoz; J. L. Ledesma; J. Rodrigo (Coordinadores), *Culturas y políticas de la violência: España siglo XX*, Madrid: Siete Mares. p. 251-278.

Ruíz Rodríguez, Ignacio (1996) - "Fuero académico em las universidades americanas en la época de los Austrias", https://ebuah.uah.es/dspace/bitstream/handle/10017/5923/Fuero%20Académico%20en%20las%20Universidades%20Americanas%20en%20la%20Época%20de%20los%20Austrias.pdf?sequence=1&isAllowed=y

Samara, Maria Alice (2009) - "O republicanismo", *História da Primeira República Portuguesa*, Coord. Fernando Rosas; Maria Fernanda Rollo. Lisboa: Tinta da China. p. 61-77.

Santos, Cândido dos (s. d.) - *A mulher e a Universidade do Porto*. Porto: Universidade do Porto, A propósito do Centenário da Formatura das Primeiras Médicas Portuguesas.

Serra, João B. (2009) - "A evolução política (1910-1917)", *História da Primeira República Portuguesa*, Coord. Fernando Rosas; Maria Fernanda Rollo. Lisboa: Tinta da China. p. 93-128.

Sigrist, Natalia Tikhonov (2009) - "Les femmes et l'université en France, 1860-1914", *Histoire de l'éducation* [En ligne], 122 | 2009: http://journals.openedition.org/histoire-education/1940 ; DOI : https://doi.org/10.4000/histoire-education.1940

Souza, José Ferreira Marnoco e (1913) - *Constituição politica da Republica Portuguêsa. Commentari*. Coimbra: F. França Amado Editor.

Torgal, Luís Reis (2010) - "A República e a instrução pública: o caso do ensino superior", *Biblos*, FLUC, VIII. p. 127-156; https://digitalis-dsp.uc.pt/bitstream/10316.2/32526/1/BiblosVIII_artigo6.pdf

Torgal, Luís Reis (2013) - "Universidade de Coimbra", *Dicionário de História da I República e do Republicanismo*, vol. III: N-Z, Lisboa: Assembleia da República. p. 1053-1060.

"Uso de capa e batina, casos que até agora eram regulados pelo fôro académico da Universidade de Coimbra" (1910), *Bibliotheca Democratica de Legislação. Periodico Jurídico*, nº 3, Anno I. p. 23; https://purl.pt/30056/4/sc-10740-4-p_PDF/sc-10740-4-p_PDF_24-C-R0150/sc-10740-4-p_0000_1-28_t24-C-R0150.pdf

Valladares Chamorro, Odalis (2012) - "La incursión de las mujeres a los estudios universitários". *CIAN-Revista De Historia De Las Universidades*, *15*(1). p. 105-123; https://e-revistas.uc3m.es/index.php/CIAN/article/view/1544

Vaquinhas, Irene (2018) - "Mulheres na Universidade de Coimbra: o caso das primeiras estudantes cabo-verdianas" / "Women at the University of Coimbra: the case of the first Cape Verdean female students", *História. Revista da FLUP*. Porto. IV Série. Vol. 8, no 1. p. 219-244; http://ojs.letras.up.pt/index.php/historia/article/viewFile/4515/4230

Vaquinhas, Irene (2019) - "História das mulheres e de género em Portugal: horizontes temáticos e desafios atuais", *Género na arte. Corpo, sexualidade, identidade, resistência, Faces de Eva. Estudos sobre a Mulher*, Lisboa: nº extra, FCS da UNL. p. 37-55. http://hdl.handle.net/10316/88149

Vaquinhas, Irene; Ribeiro, Maria Manuela Tavares (2020) - "Os estudantes da Universidade de Coimbra da reforma pombalina à implantação da República, 1772-1910 / Students of the University of Coimbra from the Pombaline Reform to the Founding of the Republic, 1772-1910 / Les étudiants de l'Université de Coimbra de la réforme pombaline à la République, 1772-1910», *Ler História*, nº 76. p. 55-79.

Vasconcelos, António de (1987) - "Génese e revolução histórica do foro académico da Universidade portuguesa; extinção do mesmo 1290-1834", *Escritos vários relativos à Universidade Dionisiana*. Reedição preparada por Manuel Augusto Rodrigues, vol. I. Coimbra: Arquivo da Universidade de Coimbra. p. 297-334.

Ventura, António (2016) - *Silêncio e virtude. Uma história da Maçonaria Feminina em Portugal (1814-1990)*, Lisboa, Temas e Debates / Círculo de Leitores.

Vicente, Ana (2009) - "Antifeminismo. A resistência ao evidente", *Dança dos Demónios*. Coord. António Marujo and José Eduardo Franco, Lisbon: Temas e Debates. p. 431-483.